Praise for
The Holy Land

"*The Holy Land Key* causes you to look over y̲o̲u̲... ...d blessing upon His people, and to look forward to the many prophecies that a.̲. yet to be fulfilled."

—DAVID JEREMIAH, founder and CEO of Turning Point
Ministries; senior pastor of Shadow Mountain Community
Church; San Diego

"Get ready for your mind to expand with new thoughts, your heart to enfold God's people, your eyes to glimpse God's plan, and your faith to soar in worship. My applause!"

—ANNE GRAHAM LOTZ, speaker; author of *The Magnificent Obsession*

"Ray Bentley has immersed himself in the land of the Book and the people of the land. His challenge to not only study prophecy but also to live it rings with the clarity of a bell. He makes an ancient subject come alive, and I found this book riveting and convicting and moving."

—JERRY B. JENKINS, coauthor of the *New York Times*
bestselling Left Behind series

"In *The Holy Land Key,* Ray Bentley ties together history, current events, prophecy, Israel's feasts and festivals, and the progress of the gospel among Jews and Arabs. Ray also explains the mystery of the Messiah's return, which God laid out for us to see through dramatic signs in the heavens. This book will challenge your thinking, fill you with hope, and bless your life."

—TOM DOYLE, vice president of e3 Partners and author
of *Dreams and Visions: Is Jesus Awakening the Muslim World?*

"Seeing prophecy through the eyes of God's chosen people, Israel, is the only way to fully understand all its implications. Ray Bentley sets forth the importance of being on God's calendar and seeing the patterns that are visible in God's feasts. Ray gives us a greater understanding of the signs in the heavens as God's signals of coming events. I am glad he is getting the truth out in these last days, as we know time is short!"

—PASTOR MARK BILTZ, founder of El Shaddai Ministries

"What I appreciate most about *The Holy Land Key* is the common ground Ray Bentley and I have in our hearts. We both desire that out of every tribe, tongue, and nation countless numbers of individuals would be saved and brought into the kingdom of Christ. I appreciate the growing interest Ray has in the perspective of Arab and Palestinian believers living in the land. We do not have to allow differences to keep us from loving each other and enjoying the wondrous friendship and fellowship Christ brings."

—BOTRUS MANSOUR, general director of Nazareth Baptist School
and author of *When Your Neighbor Is the Savior*

"*The Holy Land Key* offers a look into the heart of one who is a lover of God's people and a true friend of the Jewish people. Ray's longtime interest in God's covenant with His people, Israel, and his insatiable desire to find God's mind on the issues of the conflict in the Middle East make this book a pleasure to read."

—TASS SAADA, founder and president of Seeds of Hope
and author of *Once an Arafat Man*

THE
HOLY LAND
KEY

THE
HOLY LAND
KEY

UNLOCKING END-TIMES PROPHECY
THROUGH THE LIVES OF
GOD'S PEOPLE IN ISRAEL

RAY BENTLEY

WITH GENEVIEVE GILLESPIE

WATERBROOK
PRESS

THE HOLY LAND KEY
PUBLISHED BY WATERBROOK PRESS
12265 Oracle Boulevard, Suite 200
Colorado Springs, Colorado 80921

Trade Paperback ISBN 978-0-307-73206-4
eBook ISBN 978-0-307-73207-1

Published in the United States by WaterBrook Multnomah, an imprint of the Crown Publishing Group, a division
of Random House LLC, New York, a Penguin Random House Company.

WATERBROOK and its deer colophon are registered trademarks of Random House LLC.

The Cataloging-in-Publication Data is on file with the Library of Congress.

Printed in the United States of America
2014

10 9 8 7 6 5 4 3

SPECIAL SALES
Most WaterBrook Multnomah books are available at special quantity discounts when purchased in bulk by
corporations, organizations, and special-interest groups. Custom imprinting or excerpting can also be done
to fit special needs. For information, please e-mail SpecialMarkets@WaterBrookMultnomah.com or call
1-800-603-7051.

To my Lord and Savior, Jesus Christ
and my beautiful wife, Vicki.
And to the memory of Ron Nachman
and his beloved wife, Dorit,
who carries on his legacy.
Ron will always be the John Wayne of Israel to me—
a title I know he relished!

I also dedicate this book to Chuck Smith,
my beloved pastor,
who has gone home to the Lord.
He taught me to love God's Word
and Israel and her people.
And he ignited a whole generation of believers,
including me,
with a passion to prepare the way
for the Lord's return.
Maranatha!

CONTENTS

PART 4: GOD GIVES US SIGNS

PART 5: IT IS TIME TO STEP INTO THE PROPHETIC STORY

ACKNOWLEDGMENTS

Thank you, Lord Jesus, for speaking to me in so many wonderful ways and for all the precious people you have brought into my life as friends. I am grateful for their encouragement in my life and in publishing.

Thank you, Vicki, for being my amazing and beautiful wife. Thank you so much for encouraging me to write from my heart all we have learned together in this incredible journey. I love you so much!

Thank you, Shawn and Annie, Noah, Bentley, and Isaac; Daniel and Jill, Benjamin, Quinn, Andrew, and baby Haddyn! I am so proud of you. I thank God for my children and grandchildren. Thank you, Mom and Dad, for your faithfulness, love, and blessings from the very beginning.

Thank you to Chuck Smith, who has been my pastor since I was eighteen years of age. He is the one who taught me to teach through the Bible, to fall in love with Israel, and to bless the Jewish people. He laid the foundation for all my later discoveries and insight into the Scriptures.

Thank you to Bruce Johnston, who is the constant figure behind much of what you read in *The Holy Land Key*. He introduced me to Robert Mawire and to Ron Nachman. Bruce heads up JH Ranch in Northern California, which has helped lay the foundation for a place where Israeli exchange students can experience the love of God. He and his wife, Heather, built a protocol for the National Youth Development Center in Ariel, Israel.

Thank you to Doug Dorsey, Glenn Hirashiki, George Chial, Danny Ramos, and Sherry Ciccone for their behind-the-scenes, tireless organizing of our Israeli tours and student-exchange program and for befriending the people of Israel so graciously, paving the way for many of the connections and friends I have in Israel today.

Thank you to Andy Puterbaugh and all those who have prayed fervently that God will use this message to bring insight and open the eyes of Jesus's bride, the church, to her divine calling in blessing the Jewish people and her neighbors "for such a time as this."

Thank you to the congregation of Maranatha Chapel. You have listened as I have taught everything I am learning and have prayed faithfully for me and encouraged me in this journey. What a gift from God you have been.

Thank you to Dana Dodds, Mike Gallagher, Ron Harper, David Pepper, and Gary Priest for your unwavering support, prayers, and friendship in sharing the vision.

Thank you to Robert Mawire. Your unique background and special insight have opened doors for me into the heart of Israel and the heart of God.

I also am deeply indebted to my Jewish brothers Joel Rosenberg and Mark Biltz. Their fresh insights, wisdom, encouragement, and friendship cannot be overstated. And thank you to Tass Saada and Botrus Mansour, my Palestinian brothers who taught me to love the sons of Ishmael. And thank you to my dear friend Ron Nachman. Thank you for letting me share your incredible stories and your lives.

Thank you to Anne Graham Lotz for your passion for the Second Coming, your excitement about the gospel communicated in the stars, and your loving prayers and encouragement to get this message out to the church.

Thank you to Tom Doyle, who said, "Man, you have to get an agent and get this published!" and introduced me to my wonderful agent, David Shepherd. Thank you, David, for your great advice and guidance along the way.

A very special thank you to Ron Lee, whose brilliance in editing helped bring such clarity and focus to this project. You're the best.

Thank you to Bob and Jennie Gillespie. Jennie, you have the ability to read my mind, and your writing and editing have helped give me a voice in sharing these incredible stories, revelations, and insights into the Scriptures. I thank God for bringing both of you into my life, and I look forward to where we will go from here.

Finally, thank you to Avi Zimmerman. You are the most gracious host and advocate for Christians who are trying to help heal and build friendships between Christians and Jews. And thank you to the people of Israel, who have worked so hard to make our trips and journeys not only great tourist visits but also meaningful times of learning and friendship.

These Are the People the Prophets Saw

THE HOLY LAND KEY IS NOT A BOOK THAT RENEWS familiar debates over a prophetic time line or argues for or against a particular interpretation of John's Revelation. We will not try to narrow down the most likely candidates for the Antichrist. It is important to read prophecy carefully, to handle its interpretation with great care, and to anchor all our conclusions in God's Word, but we also want to explore some new territories in Scripture that have prophetic significance.

In the chapters that follow, we will look at certain passages of Scripture from a Hebrew perspective. We also will study what God has written in the heavens and what the Bible says about these heavenly revelations. We will look at the testimony of history, we will study the Jewish calendar and the biblical feasts, and we will even find startling insights based on research done by NASA on blood moons.

Paul wrote in Romans 1 that we are without excuse if we fail to see God and His character in the signs that are clear in His creation. God has left signs for us in more places than we can imagine. It would be a mistake to ignore any of them.

God's Covenant with His Chosen People

One of the clearest and most enduring signs is God's unbroken relationship with the Jewish people. The people living today in the Holy Land are the people the ancient prophets saw in the end times. They are the descendants of Jesus's family and of His disciples. They are living evidence of God's plan to gather His people back to Israel after two thousand years of exile.

Israel is a witness to the world. It is not an exaggeration to say that when we look at Israel, we are looking into the eyes of God. When we look at Israel, we see God's intentions for the world. We will explore this further in the chapters that follow.

We also will look at patterns throughout history that open our eyes to what the very near future holds. Some of the patterns that most clearly reveal God's plans as well as His heart are found in the Hebrew calendar and the timing of the feasts of the Lord listed in Scripture. The significance of these Jewish holidays is far greater today than was the original purpose of each feast.

Further, it has been revealed that the timing of the feasts—right down to the specific dates—coincides with repeated cycles of astronomical events and patterns. The full meaning of this correlation remains to be seen, but it is significant that God confirms the testimony of history, of the Scriptures, of religious observance, and of the signs He has put in the heavens. All these together point to the coming—and the return—of the promised Messiah. Ultimately, they point to Israel's destiny and to the destiny of humanity. The Jews were given the predictions of the ancient prophets long before the Christians inherited those Scriptures along with the New Covenant of God's Word. It is important to look carefully at the way Jews understand the written testimony of the Hebrew prophets. Familiar prophecies from thousands of years ago are being fulfilled today in Israel. It is no overstatement to say that God's plan is being moved forward by committed Jews, and this, too, is a revelation to us.

God called Israel the "apple of His eye" (Zechariah 2:8). That never has changed, and when God looks at His chosen people today, He sees His plans unfolding at the end of this age. When we look at Israel, we see God's intentions for the world. I will introduce you to modern-day Israelis who—no matter if they are Jewish or Gentile, Christian or otherwise—are answering the call of God on their lives. These current-day brothers and sisters of Jesus have much to show us of the ways and the heart of God.

But the people of Israel and their work to restore the Holy Land is only a start.

In addition, we will look at the signs of what God will bring to pass on earth. This includes a study of the heavens, the way time is recorded, and more. A guiding principle here is to identify and learn from patterns that are repeated throughout Scripture and described in 1 Corinthians 15:46: "However, the spiritual is not first, but the natural, and afterward the spiritual." What God does in the natural realm is a picture of what He is doing in the spiritual realm. God reveals His plans and His future work, including what is in store at the end of the age, first in the natural world.

Bringing Prophecy to Life

Prophecy and its interpretation are a fascinating study. You can get lost in the words of God's ancient messengers, studying their dreams and visions and seeking to piece together the larger picture. It is important to know what God has said through His prophets. However, we need to avoid the tendency to study prophecy with a sort of academic detachment that separates us emotionally—and spiritually—from the impact of what God is doing on earth. Prophecy is a biblical teaching to be lived out. We need to bring prophecy to life by connecting it to our lives and the lives of others.

By getting to know people who live in the Holy Land (Jews, Christians, Israeli Arabs, and Palestinians), we are drawn into more than just the facts of prophecy. We go beyond end-times theories and encounter the people who are involved in the fulfillment of prophecy. These descendants of Jesus are witnessing events He prophesied when He lived in the same land two thousand years ago.

More and more, Christians are taking action by joining with God's people of Israel. The Israelis witness daily what God is doing in their ancestral land. They are eyewitnesses to the unfolding of God's work. You and I—and all people of faith who join with Israel in an active way—are part of the prophetic story. A Jewish friend who helped me go much deeper in my study and understanding of prophecy opened my eyes to this truth.

Ron Nachman, the mayor of a small Israeli city in the West Bank, took great risks to help rebuild Israel after the Jews started returning to their homeland after

1948. He read the Hebrew prophets and studied the ways their visions were becoming reality in the Holy Land—the land he was committed to help restore.

Men such as Ron see the solidarity of Christians who work alongside Israelis as an important sign of prophecy being fulfilled. The people living in Israel are already on the scene of God's culminating work on earth: the return of His Son to claim His own. As God brings this age to a close, Israelis are having their eyes opened to God's dealings with humanity. It is not simply the building of a nation, protecting Israel against the enemies that surround it, or arguing the issues related to territory and boundaries as part of the so-called Palestinian question. All those are important, of course, but there is a growing sense that developments are taking place that transcend political, military, and nationalistic concerns. These are spiritual issues and spiritual concerns shared by Jews, Arabs, and Christians alike.

For years we have seen the Arab-Israeli conflict dominate the headlines. As I was writing this book, Israel was criticized for sending aircraft into Syria to destroy missiles supplied by Iran and stored near Damascus. The missiles were said to have a two-hundred-mile range and were en route to Hezbollah fighters. Hezbollah, a sworn enemy of Israel, typically operates in Lebanon but also has joined the fighting in Syria's civil war.[1] Global tensions have focused in and around Israel since the rebirth of the Jewish state in 1948. Just about everything concerning Israel—even its right to exist—remains the focus of international debate in spite of decades of negotiations, wars, shifting boundaries, and treaties.

What Are Israelis Hearing from God?

Many of the signposts we have missed in our past study of prophecy come clearly into view only when we study Scripture in tandem with committed Israelis. How do the people of Israel read the signs of the times? What do they anticipate for the future as they face the hostility of enemies bent on their destruction?

To study prophecy apart from the people who live in the Holy Land is similar to studying a road atlas and pretending you've visited the Grand Canyon or Yosemite National Parks. Reading words on a page is only one of the steps in learning the deeper meaning of prophecy. The prophets delivered their prophecies to people who needed to have their eyes and hearts opened to God's plans. None of this has changed since the days of Isaiah and Jeremiah. God has not changed His plans, nor has He stopped speaking to His people—as we will see.

Many of the people I am working with in Israel are hearing from God. He is opening the eyes of His people to the reality of His power, His involvement in world affairs, His never-ending love for His people, and His plans. He is setting things in order to bring about His kingdom on earth, just as His prophets foretold.

In *The Holy Land Key* you will be introduced to contemporary Israelis—from national leaders to local leaders to ordinary citizens. You will begin to hear from God just as those in Israel hear from Him. Let's start making introductions.

PART I

A More Complete Way to Study Prophecy

Partnering with Those Who Are Helping to Fulfill Prophecy

It was winter in 1977. A helicopter hovered over a desolate patch of land in the Samarian wilderness. The downdraft created by the aircraft's blades churned up dirt, thrashed the brown shrubs, and muted the pilot's bellowed instructions.

On the ground below, a man watched the copter descend and guided it to a safe landing. Two civilians and ten Israel Defense Forces (IDF) soldiers gathered behind the man on the ground. When the aircraft landed, the soldiers scrambled to secure the supplies and equipment they needed to survive in this harsh environment. The helicopter then lifted off and sped away.

Alone now on a barren hilltop dusted with snow, the men pitched two tents. The small band set up camp in what is regarded by the rest of the world as disputed territory. But in the mind of the man who guided the helicopter to a safe landing, this area had been claimed for Israel thousands of years earlier. He and his partners were here to found a city that would be named in honor of the sacred city, Jerusalem. This new settlement would be known as Ariel, meaning "lion of God."

In the 1970s the Cold War had the world locked in its grip, and Egyptian president Anwar Sadat made an unprecedented journey to Jerusalem, setting off another round of Middle East peace talks. Frank Zappa and Elton John were singing about

Jesus Freaks, and the best-selling book of the decade had declared an epitaph for our planet: *The Late Great Planet Earth*. It was a time of turmoil and instability, and no region of the world was more contested than the territory of the small nation of Israel.

The city of Ariel began as a campground on heavily disputed land. The gutsy families who lived there hauled in water and relied on their own generators for power. A weekly caravan brought in supplies. The emerging city enraged Palestinians and divided Jews, who were not unanimous in supporting Israeli settlements in contested regions.

Nearly a quarter century later, I stayed in the city of Ariel in a hotel that boasted a large crater in its front lobby, the result of a suicide terrorist attack that failed to demolish its target. The land surrounding the hotel should have been barren, having once been empty desert. But in 2001 I could see that the surrounding earth was rich, the new vines were green, and the hotel shimmered with pools and fountains.

Earlier that day I had knelt in the dirt of a vineyard and planted grapevines. The sun warmed my back, but the realization of what I was doing rushed through me with a different kind of warmth. Soldiers in camouflage uniforms stood nearby, their weapons at ease. They were young and appeared to be relaxed. But I knew they were highly trained members of one of the best armies in the world, ready at any moment to defend the land of their heritage.

I am one of many pilgrims who have taken part in the ceremony of planting a vineyard in Ariel. Working the soil and adding new vines to this vineyard somehow helped to clarify a number of issues for me. Ariel is not part of what the world community considers to be Israel. It stands in a hotly disputed area known to the rest of the world as the West Bank. Most Israelis identify this area as Judea and Samaria, part of ancient Israel and now considered part of modern Israel as well. It is a contested region where war could erupt at any moment.

In the heart of this hostile area, a man who had the ruggedness and courage of John Wayne arrived to found a city. That's how it seemed to me, anyway. Ron Nachman is the man who put his life on the line many times, a man who became my close friend. He was proud to be seen as the John Wayne of Israel. The people of Ariel elected him as mayor for four terms. He is one of the reasons I love Israel.

The life-changing visit to Ariel opened my eyes to the deeper meaning of what God is doing in the world. For me, Israel is no longer just a reference point for a prophetic timetable. I have loved the study of prophecy since I was a teenager, but now the people of Israel make prophecy come alive.

As my friendship with Mayor Nachman deepened, we discussed Scripture and prophecy. He saw Scripture as being fulfilled through the homecoming of so many Jews to Israel, which had begun in earnest after Resolution 181 was adopted by the United Nations General Assembly in late 1947. From all over the globe, Jews continue to uproot their lives and resettle in Israel, sometimes at great personal sacrifice.

This near-mythical nation whose story is told in Scripture and history had been removed from the earth, its people taken into exile through a series of deportations. Jews were taken captive to Assyria, Persia, and Babylon and then scattered to the four corners of the globe. No other nation on earth has ceased to exist, with its people dispersed for so long, only to be reborn as a nation on its original land. That, in itself, is a miracle.

A New Awareness of an Age-Old Conflict

After my life-changing visit to Ariel in 2001, I caught a flight to meet my family in Hawaii. Shortly after I awoke the following morning, the phone in our hotel room rang. I answered it, and a good friend in Maui said something I didn't catch at first. She seemed to be losing control of her emotions.

"Turn on the television," she said. "Now!" She was barely able to get the words out, but I heard her say, "We're being attacked."

It was September 11. Four commercial jetliners had been hijacked by Al Qaeda terrorists and used as deadly weapons against American citizens. We began checking with other friends and traveling companions. Several of the team members who had traveled with us to Israel had left there on a later flight. They had landed in Newark,

New Jersey, and were stranded on the tarmac. They saw smoke billowing from lower Manhattan. Many of them ended up hitchhiking home across the country.

With this direct attack on US soil, planned and executed by Islamic radicals, everything changed. A new awareness of an age-old conflict changed how we thought about Islam, the Arab nations, and the Jewish state. Even though the attack was launched against New York City and Washington DC, Israel was the key. The terrorists hated its existence and hated the United States for supporting the Jewish state.

Just days earlier, when I was planting vines in Ariel, the importance of God's people in Israel had been brought home to me. I had studied prophecy for decades, but on that afternoon I knew the fate of the world revolved around Israel. I had come face to face with a new understanding of prophecy and how God has chosen to open our eyes to His work on earth. It is not just the geography of Israel that is important to our understanding. To get the clearest picture of what God is doing, it helps to read prophecy through the eyes of the people who live in Israel today.

Israel and her people are the center of our world, our history, and our future.

Joining Today's Developments in an Ancient Story

I WAS ELEVEN YEARS OLD WHEN I STARTED SEEING newspaper headlines about Israel's miraculous victory over Egypt, Jordan, and Syria in 1967. Israel had captured the Gaza Strip, the Golan Heights, the West Bank, and, most important, the Old City of Jerusalem. The war lasted just six days.

As the years passed, I continued to read news reports about Israel, and the ancient land of the Bible took on flesh and bones. Israel was emerging from the pages of Scripture and becoming a real, living nation. My parents had less time to keep up with the latest news from the Middle East. They were raising three sons at a time when the United States was involved in its own war in Southeast Asia. Many of my friends were protesting the war, using drugs, and exploring the counterculture. I wanted to be a radical too—but I was becoming convinced that the gospel of Jesus was the most radical message ever. It was the message that would turn social conventions upside down.

My music hero was Larry Norman, one of the original Jesus People. He sang, "I wish we'd all been ready," and I felt as if I needed to pull people out of a burning building. In high school, fueled by my love for God and His Word, my growing knowledge of prophecy, and my consuming interest in Israel, I started a Bible study. Even then I was convinced that Israel was at the center of what God was doing on earth. I knew somehow that the biblical prophecies would be fulfilled very soon, perhaps in my lifetime.

I realized I needed a teacher, someone who was knowledgeable and also burned with passion for God, the gospel, and Israel. I found that teacher in Chuck Smith, founding pastor of Calvary Chapel in Costa Mesa, California.

Chuck already had a growing number of young people eager to soak in his teaching. It didn't matter that he was a balding, middle-aged man.

He would teach while sitting on a stool, his rapt listeners surrounding him, some lying facedown on the floor, others sprawled on the floor, the stage, and in the pews. I first heard about Chuck when my mom showed me an article about him in *Look* magazine describing the Jesus People. By then, the early 1970s, the media had found a good story in the Jesus Movement. One *Los Angeles Times* reporter described Pastor Chuck as a person "who possessed 'a big smile so full of peace that you had to resent it.'"[1]

I studied the magazine photographs, which showed my generation raising their hands to worship God, singing with guitars and drums in church, flocking to the shores of the Pacific Ocean to be baptized. For the early 1970s this was revolutionary.

During my senior year of high school, Pastor Chuck came to San Diego to speak, and I was eager to hear this man some were calling "the pied piper of the Jesus generation."[2] I had felt the tug toward ministry and was making plans to attend a Wesleyan seminary in Oklahoma. But then I heard Chuck teach verse by verse from John 7. He preached from the entire gospel, using all the scriptures—not just a few select verses. Then he read from the words of Jesus: "If any man thirst, let him come unto me, and drink. He that believeth on me, as the scripture hath said, out of his belly shall flow rivers of living water" (John 7:37–38, KJV). In that moment I experienced what John Wesley described: "I felt my heart strangely warmed."[3]

Afterward, when I asked Chuck what seminary he had attended, he didn't tell me. Instead, he said I could start going through the Bible verse by verse at his church, Calvary Chapel of Costa Mesa. He invited me to live at the House of Psalms, and so I decided to live in a commune rather than attend seminary. I became a Nazarene/Wesleyan/Jesus Freak.

I moved into the House of Psalms right out of high school. Arriving with my duffel bag and backpack, I stepped into a scene I had read about and had watched from afar. Pouring into the communal houses were barefoot, unbathed hippies, runaways, and throwaways—young people from the streets, from homes where families no longer tolerated them, from other communes. With their long, matted hair, overalls, and bell-bottom jeans, some were grungy and unkempt, and others were swathed in wild hues of psychedelic colors. They had fringe and bells sewn into the hems of their clothing, looking very much like the flower children they had been dubbed. Some were hardened, bitter, angry, strung out, and recovering from destructive lifestyles. Others were idealistic visionaries who found peace in Jesus as well as a catalyst for their hopes and dreams.

I knew I was part of a great movement. I saw miracles. I saw people transformed. I witnessed hippies and conservatives working together. The beach baptisms were beautiful, with thousands of young people singing, worshiping, and being healed of the hurts and pains of the world. The sun would set into the Pacific Ocean at the end of a service, and we would sit on the sand in the fading light, watching the silhouettes of new converts come out of the ocean. We were in awe of what God was doing.

As I studied under Chuck Smith, I took to heart the truths that thousands of years ago God chose a people to bear witness to the nations. Two thousand years ago the Jewish Messiah came to earth, fulfilling the Law and the Prophets. But God's work on earth was not complete, and His promise to the Jews stands forever.

This ancient history, preserved for us in the Bible, is much more than just a record of Semitic peoples and their migrations in the ancient Near East. It also is a description of the tension within the family of Abraham that set in motion the strife, bitterness, and conflict that have never found resolution. Instead, the divisions have deepened, fed by thousands of years of hatred, misunderstanding, and war.

Ancient Origins of the Arab-Israeli Conflict

People who are not familiar with the Bible might assume the tensions in the Middle East date back to UN Resolution 181, the decision by the international body to approve the creation of a Jewish state as well as an Arab state. While many Jews had remained in the land, living alongside Palestinians, most of the world's Jewish population had spent nearly two thousand years in exile. With the UN action, the Jews finally were granted a homeland. When they began to return in large numbers from the Diaspora (the dispersion of Jewish people, scattered in exile), the land of Palestine erupted in violence.

The Arabs who had occupied the territory for two millennia resisted the UN action, and skirmishes followed. But the Israelis were committed to restoring their homeland. And since 1948, as Israel has flourished, regional tensions have similarly escalated between Jews and Arabs. The tensions date back four thousand years to the story of Abraham and his sons.

Abraham, originally known as Abram, was called to leave his home in Ur. God told him to set out with his family on a journey in search of a different land. So Abram sojourned toward Canaan, waiting for God to let him know when he had reached the land of promise. It is one of the greatest stories of faith in the Bible. It also reveals the terrible mistakes made by a man of faith toward his sons and the seeds of bitterness and conflict that were sown.

Rejecting a Son

The old man wept as he watched his son walk, head down, into the desert. The boy's mother reached out to support her son, but the boy angrily pushed her hand away. Abraham ached as he saw the mother's stricken expression. But then the boy took the waterskin and the bread wrapped in cloth that his mother had been carrying, shouldered them, and reached for her arm as if to reassure her with his youthful strength.

Abraham longed to call them back, needing to absolve his guilt and sorrow. *Don't let him die,* he pleaded. God had promised, "I will also make a nation of the son of the bondwoman, because he is your seed" (Genesis 21:13). The old man repeated the promise, clinging to it as he watched his son and the son's mother, Hagar, walk off into the barren land.

Abraham could see anger in his son Ishmael. The father stared, willing Ishmael to look back one last time, but the boy was angry and stubborn. He refused to acknowledge his father. Watching the two figures gradually disappear in the distance, Abraham prayed to God. "Bless him," he whispered. "May he always know Your presence." Then Abraham turned and slowly walked home to his other son, Isaac. He was the rightful heir of God's promise to Abraham, the one chosen by God to play a unique role in the story of the human race, the one who would build a nation that would bring forth the Messiah.

The conflict that dominates not just the Middle East but the entire world began with that story. The first shot of bitterness into the heart of future Arab nations and the first pain of isolation and sacrifice that birthed the nation of Israel were felt as Ishmael disappeared into the desert, banished by his father.

When I was growing up, the Cold War was fought against the threat of communism, which loomed constantly on the horizon. Both the democratic West and the communist USSR possessed enough nuclear warheads to destroy the earth. We knew that nuclear missiles were aimed at the United States, ready to destroy us. But even after the collapse of the Soviet threat, we still face international tensions that could erupt at any moment and draw so many nations into war. The initial warring parties will be the descendants of Ishmael, the father of the nations we know today as Arab, and the descendants of Isaac, who carried on the promise God gave to Abraham and eventually resulted in the nation of Israel. The bitter rivalry between these brothers is played out in threats, rocket attacks, suicide bombers, UN condemnations, negotiations, treaties, and increasing acts of terrorism.

Abraham's lack of faith generated a deep animosity between his sons that continues to this day. The story is told in the book of Genesis.

The Tale of Two Brothers

God had promised Abraham and his wife, Sarah, a son in their old age (see Genesis 15:1–18:15). But as the couple saw the years spin by, Sarah grew impatient. She asked Abraham to sleep with her maidservant, Hagar, and the result was a son named Ishmael. Through no fault of his own, Ishmael was not the promised son, and his presence distressed Sarah, which caused a disturbance in the whole household. Abraham tried to fix things by pleading for what was tangible: the son who already existed. "If only Ishmael might live under your blessing!" he cried. But God said, "No, Sarah your wife shall bear you a son, and you shall call his name Isaac; I will establish My covenant with him for an everlasting covenant, and with his descendants after him" (Genesis 17:19).

God kept His promise. In spite of her old age, Sarah gave birth to Isaac, the promised seed from whom God pledged to forge a great nation: Israel. The chosen people would face persecution, captivity, exile, destruction, and yet rise from the ashes to be reborn in modern times.

Abraham loved Ishmael as well, and God responded to the firstborn son with a promise all his own: "Behold, I have blessed him, and will make him fruitful, and will multiply him exceedingly. He shall beget twelve princes, and I will make him a great nation. But My covenant I will establish with Isaac, whom Sarah shall bear to you at this set time next year" (Genesis 17:20–21). While Isaac carried the promise that resulted in the nation of Israel and the Jewish faith, from Ishmael came the Arab nations, out of which sprang the prolific Muslim faith. Most sources estimate the Muslim population at between 1.5 billion and 1.7 billion, making up 23 percent of the world's population.[4]

Throughout history Ishmael's descendants have felt cheated, being the nations that Abraham exiled to the desert. Today the rest of the world waits and watches, wondering what will happen to Israel, a small nation surrounded by enemies committed to its destruction.

A Second Tale of Two Brothers

Centuries after Ishmael's banishment, Jesus told a story about two sons and a hurting father. Like Abraham, this father loved both his sons, and like Abraham, the father had to treat his two sons differently. We meet the prodigal son and his older brother in Luke 15. The prodigal left home, tried to lose his identity, squandered his father's blessings, and ended up in a pigpen. The older brother remained home, working hard to earn what he already possessed: his father's love and blessing.

Perhaps we can understand through this story how God the Father views the descendants of Isaac (the Jews) and the descendants of Ishmael (the Arabs). Like the prodigal son, the children of Israel ran away from their Father again and again. Throughout the Bible the Israelites are called beloved and chosen. They also are described as unruly, stubborn, and rebellious (see Deuteronomy 9:6–10). After Moses delivered them from slavery in Egypt, they wandered for forty years in the Sinai desert because of their disobedience. And even after the Lord brought them into the Promised Land, they still turned to idols.

The Hebrews eventually occupied Canaan. They built a nation that was recognized—and sometimes feared—by the world powers of that era. Their two greatest kings (David and Solomon) consolidated wealth, commerce, military might, and the worship of God. But the glory of Israel was short lived. After Solomon's death, the nation split into two kingdoms: Judah (the southern tribes) and Israel (the northern tribes). For the most part, the kings of the two kingdoms turned their backs on God, and the nations grew weaker. In 722 BC the Assyrians conquered the northern kingdom and scattered these ten tribes throughout the empire.

After more than a century of political wars were fought to control Judah, the southern kingdom fell to Babylon around 597 BC. Nebuchadnezzar deported approximately ten thousand Jews to his capital, beginning what is called in Jewish history the Exile.[5]

Thus the Israelites were forcibly removed from the Holy Land and taken to foreign lands. No longer was there a sovereign nation of Israel. The loss of their ancestral home brings to mind the younger son of the loving father in Jesus's parable. After squandering his inheritance, the prodigal found himself sleeping with swine.

Israel's rebellion grieved God, and He sent prophets to warn them, seeking to restore the broken relationship. Jesus tells us in His story that on a certain day, after the prodigal had squandered everything, he "came to himself" (Luke 15:17). The disgraced son returned home, disheveled and downcast from working in pigpens and foraging for food. As the disgraced son trudged up the road toward his former home, even when he "was still a great way off, his father saw him and had compassion, and ran and fell on his neck and kissed him" (verse 20).

The father did not ask his son to clean up in order to wash away the stench of his rebellious life. This is the same ardent love that God the Father has for the Jewish people as they stream back to the Holy Land. After exile, slavery, and the Diaspora, Jews returned from around the world to the land God promised to Abraham some four thousand years earlier.

But Israel's history is only part of the story. There is Ishmael, the older brother, and his offspring, the Arabs. They never left the land. Abraham sent Ishmael and his mother into the desert, and they stayed. But like the loyal older brother in Jesus's parable, Ishmael's descendants have seethed with anger and jealousy whenever Israel receives any favor. Why would God continue to bless the descendants of this faithless people? Just as in the parable, the younger son, who appears to have done about everything wrong, receives the Father's full blessing. The older brother was loyal and stayed home, and he was angry and confused. Why would his father act this way toward the rebellious younger brother? The older brother felt he had never brought shame to the family. Why did the foolish, rebellious son deserve such an extravagant welcome?

The older brother was blind to the truth that he also had failed his father. The responsible brother served, not out of love, but out of obligation, seeking to earn his inheritance. Yet his father loved him, responding to his bitterness with, "Son, you are always with me, and all that I have is yours.… [F]or your brother was dead and is alive again, and was lost and is found" (verses 31–32).

Isaac and Ishmael Meet Again

Let's go back to the story of Abraham's two sons, Isaac and Ishmael. After being separated for decades, the brothers reunited at the touching scene of Abraham's death: "Then Abraham breathed his last and died in a good old age…and was gathered to his people. And his sons Isaac and Ishmael buried him in the cave of Machpelah" (Genesis 25:8–9).

Everything they had fought over and thought so important, all the hurt and resentment, was meaningless. Momentary peace blessed Abraham's burial. In the end they were just two boys, now grown men, who shared a father who had left a legacy of a personal relationship with God. He will forever be known as the friend of God. And now, finally, maybe his sons could learn to become friends.

There will never be peace in the Holy Land until the descendants of Isaac and Ishmael, the Jews and the Arabs, look back and realize to whom they belong. Looking at the tension in the Middle East today, it does not appear that the two sides are any closer to a shared inheritance from the same loving Father.

The study of prophecy, as well as Israel's history and the ongoing story of God's chosen people, convinced me that I had to be more than a student of God's Word. I wanted to be a part of what He is doing, a *participant* in the unfolding prophecy. I understood that Israel is people—not just a prophetic clock on the wall, revealing a prophecy timetable. I longed to connect with her people and share their joy as God reveals Himself to all of us.

But how does a pastor from San Diego do that? For me, it took an unlikely encounter with a Christian from Africa, a man who had received a specific message from God to be given to a national leader of Israel. The preacher from Africa is named Robert Mawire.

Bruce Johnston, who runs JH Ranch, a youth camp in Northern California that is involved with Israeli students, told me, "I know someone who loves Israel more than you do." And then he introduced me to Robert.

Meeting Robert dominoed into meetings with one character after another, each one pulling me deeper into this passion for Israel and her people. It was like jumping onto a fast-moving train and just trying to hold on. But after almost twenty years of traveling to Israel, meeting with leaders and ordinary citizens, and hearing and witnessing how God is at work among His people, I realized there is no other way to study God's Word than to be engaged in His work as well.

God's Covenant with Abraham Remains Fully in Force

WHEN ISRAELIS FIGHT FOR THEIR LAND AND THEIR nation's right to exist, their convictions are founded in a four-thousand-year-old contract between God and one man, Abram, the son of Terah of Ur, a tenth descendant of Noah (see Genesis 11:27–12:3). God spoke to this man while he was living in the land of the Chaldeans, which is present-day Iraq. Abram lived in a pagan land, and there was no reason he should listen to the One True God, and there was even less reason for him to obey what God told him to do:

> Get out of your country,
> From your family
> And from your father's house,
> To a land that I will show you.
> I will make you a great nation;
> I will bless you
> And make your name great;
> And you shall be a blessing.
> I will bless those who bless you,

And I will curse him who curses you;

And in you all the families of the earth shall be blessed.

      (Genesis 12:1–3)

Abram had amassed wealth and was living comfortably in Ur. It represented everything he was familiar with, and it was the home of his extended family. Any rational human in these circumstances—hearing a voice telling you to pull up stakes and start wandering with no predetermined destination—would assume you were just imagining things. But not Abram. He believed he was hearing from God and he obeyed.

"So," the story continues, "Abram departed as the LORD had spoken to him" (verse 4). Taking his nephew Lot, Abram left the land of his father at age seventy-five. He journeyed to Canaan with his wife, Sarai, and their household. Abram would later be renamed Abraham, and the contract God established with him is what we refer to as the *Abrahamic Covenant,* the foundation upon which *all* the promises of God are anchored.

Covenant Is About Relationship

A covenant is an agreement between two parties. There are two kinds of covenants: conditional and unconditional. A conditional covenant depends on both parties fulfilling certain conditions. If either person fails to carry out his or her responsibilities, the covenant is broken.

An unconditional covenant is also an agreement between two parties, but only one of the two promises to do something. Nothing is required of the other. The Abrahamic Covenant is unconditional.

God established a covenant relationship with Abram, promising to bless him. God initiated the covenant, He changed Abram's name to Abraham, and He declared that Abraham would be the father not only of the Jewish people but also of many nations.

These promises were not based on Abraham's goodness, abilities, or anticipated performance but rather God's grace. God did not choose Abraham and decide to bless him based on anything Abraham did. Yes, Abraham responded to God's call. But God made His promises before Abraham did anything. There is no evidence that Abraham did a single thing to receive the promises.

Look at the ways in which this agreement, with that unlikely beginning, has affected the world. Robert Mawire, an African Christian who looms large in what is happening in Israel today, writes: "Humankind has been perplexed by the Jewish claim to divine election. What does it mean to be a chosen people? Are the Jews above all other peoples and nations? The notion that one people among all peoples, tribes, and languages claims a definitive and futuristic messianic domination was incomprehensible to the ancient world.... [A]nd it's been a constant agitation on the world stage."[1]

This helps explain the Jews suffering persecution for thousands of years. But even with the rest of the world resisting the idea that God would choose one man and from him create a nation and a people of God's own choosing, God never has reneged on His promise. Isaac Newton, one of the great scientists and scholars in history, wrote more than three hundred years ago that the Jews would return to the Holy Land in the last days. Christopher Columbus, the explorer who believed he could reach the Far East by sailing westward and circumnavigating the globe, set out on his famous mission with a vision to help rebuild the temple in Jerusalem. (You might be surprised to learn why in a later chapter.)

But mostly, other nations have betrayed God's people rather than take God's covenant seriously. Few of God's promises have been rejected by skeptics with as much disdain as this one: "I will give you the land of Canaan as your special possession" (Psalm 105:11, NLT). But God's gift of Canaan to the Hebrews finally was recognized by an international body, the United Nations, in 1948. At that time Christians took a new interest in Israel not just as an ancient people but as a living remnant of God's covenant. Christians began to understand what the apostle Paul wrote regarding the Abrahamic Covenant: "Now it was not written for his sake alone...but also for us" (Romans 4:23–24).

Covenant Means "To Cut"

The Abrahamic Covenant was expanded when the Lord came to Abraham in a vision saying, "Do not be afraid, Abram. I am your shield, your exceedingly great reward" (Genesis 15:1). But Abraham cried out to God, "Look, You have given me no offspring" (verse 3). How could Abraham become the father of a great nation and bequeath his land and blessings (see Genesis 12:2) when he was childless and Sarah was barren? In his culture, children were a sign of God's blessing. Having no children implied a lack of blessing, of somehow being forsaken by God. The perceived shame of barrenness was painful.

Then God led Abram outside and said, " 'Look now toward heaven, and count the stars if you are able to number them.... So shall your descendants be....' And he believed in the LORD, and He accounted it to him for righteousness" (Genesis 15:5–6). God's promise was unconditional, but in Genesis 15 Abraham responded, and a relationship began to grow between them.

When Abraham asked for confirmation of the Lord's promise, God instructed him to bring before Him several animals to sacrifice. Abraham cut a heifer, a goat, a ram, a turtledove, and a pigeon in two, down the middle, with the opposite pieces facing each other. "When the sun went down and it was dark...there appeared a smoking oven and a burning torch that passed between those pieces. On the same day the LORD made a covenant with Abram, saying: 'To your descendants I have given this land, from the river of Egypt to the great river, the River Euphrates' " (Genesis 15:17–18).

The Hebrew word for *covenant* means "to cut," as in a sacrifice. The root word is "to select or to choose." God chose to love Abraham. God is always the Initiator. He sets the order of how the relationship will develop.

In Genesis 15 the smoking oven and burning torch represent God. He passed between the pieces of the sacrifice—alone. Abraham didn't walk through the sacrifices; the Lord did. In fact, "a deep sleep fell upon Abram" (verse 12), during which God spoke to him concerning the future of His people. God reiterated His promise:

"To your descendants I have given this land" (verse 18). God alone passed through the sacrifice because fulfillment of this covenant falls upon God alone. His covenant is unconditional.

This is what the Israelis are fighting for today—the fulfillment of the Abrahamic Covenant—and many of them don't even realize it. But some, including many key leaders, realize that the struggle to defend the sovereignty of Israel is more than a matter of national loyalty or engaging in geopolitical conflict. Israel is a promise from God to the world. Israel is the key to God's blessing and a witness of promises He intends to keep.

The Constitution of God's Kingdom

The Abrahamic Covenant is essentially the constitution of the kingdom of God, defining three types of promises made to Abraham:

- The promise of the land

"To a land that I will show you" (Genesis 12:1). "Then the Lord your God will bring you to the land which your fathers possessed, and you shall possess it" (Deuteronomy 30:5).

- The promise of descendants through whom the Messiah would come

The Lord said He would make of Abram a great nation (Genesis 12:2). The promise of a Messiah was repeated in God's covenant with David: "I will set up your seed after you, who will come from your body, and I will establish his kingdom.... Your throne shall be established forever" (2 Samuel 7:12, 16).

- The promise of blessing and redemption ultimately fulfilled through the Messiah, Jesus

"And in you all the families of the earth shall be blessed" (Genesis 12:3). "Behold, the days are coming, says the LORD, when I will make a new covenant with the house of Israel and with the house of Judah" (Jeremiah 31:31). "Then He said to them, 'With fervent desire I have desired to eat this Passover with you....' Then He took the cup, and gave thanks.... And He took bread, gave thanks and broke it" (Luke 22:15, 17, 19).

Establishing the Worship of the One True God

When Abraham arrived in Canaan he could not take possession of the land because Canaanites had already settled there. But he possessed the land in a different way: he established the worship of the One True God.

He didn't go into the land with conquest and war in mind. He simply traveled through the territory and, on significant occasions, stopped to build altars. He lived as a sojourner among the Canaanites and their religious practices. However, the act of building an altar was a powerful testimony—and a different way of taking possession.

The First Altar at Shechem

Shechem is one of the oldest settlements in Canaan, dating back at least four thousand years.[2] Shechem is the first place Abraham, Sarah, and Lot stopped in Canaan. It also is where God confirmed the covenant He had first made in Haran regarding the possession of the land. Abram built his first altar at Shechem:

> Abram passed through the land to the place of Shechem, as far as the terebinth tree of Moreh. And the Canaanites were then in the land. Then the LORD appeared to Abram and said, "To your descendants I will give this land." And there he built an altar to the LORD, who had appeared to him. (Genesis 12:6–7)

Later Abraham's grandson Jacob bought land from the Canaanites in Shechem. He pitched his tent and built an altar there (see Genesis 33:18–20). The bones of

Joseph, son of Jacob, were brought to Shechem from Egypt and buried in Jacob's plot (see Joshua 24:32), as were Joseph's sons Manasseh and Ephraim. Today Shechem is called Nablus by the Arabs, a transfer from Flavia Neapolis, the name given to it by the Romans in AD 72.

The Second Altar at Bethel

Abram left Shechem and moved to the mountain east of Bethel, where he built a second altar and "called on the name of the LORD" (Genesis 12:8). Eventually famine drove Abram, his family, and Lot to seek help farther south, in Egypt. Later, when he returned from Egypt as a wealthy man, he came back to Bethel, the site of his second altar. "And there Abram called on the name of the LORD" again (Genesis 13:4). Thereafter, Bethel became a significant site for Abram and his descendants.

Abraham's grandson Jacob later visited Bethel. Jacob fled to Bethel when he was seeking safety from the wrath of his brother, Esau. Using a stone for a pillow, he fell asleep and dreamed of a ladder with multitudes of angels ascending and descending from heaven to earth. The Lord spoke to Jacob: "I am the LORD God of Abraham your father and the God of Isaac; the land on which you lie I will give to you and your descendants.... Behold, I am with you and will keep you wherever you go, and will bring you back to this land; for I will not leave you until I have done what I have spoken to you" (Genesis 28:13, 15). When Jacob awoke, he anointed with oil the stone on which he had slept and named the place Bethel, meaning "the house of God."

Later, again in desperation, Jacob returned to Bethel (see Genesis 35:1). Jacob built his own altar, separate from Abraham's original altar, and named it El Bethel (see verse 7). Soon after, God changed Jacob's name to Israel, promising "a company of nations shall proceed from you, and kings shall come from your body" (verse 11).

The Third Altar at Hebron

Abram and Lot had grown wealthy, possessing vast flocks and herds. Because of the livestock and the size of their combined families, the land could no longer support them both. Abram generously let Lot pick where he would settle, and Lot chose the richest land. That left Abram to move his caravan to the hills of Canaan.

I can picture Abram watching Lot leave, his long caravan receding into the distance while Abram stood in Canaan, perhaps sad to see his family divided by distance. And then he heard a familiar voice: "Lift your eyes now...for all the land which you see I give to you and your descendants forever. And I will make your descendants as the dust of the earth; so that if a man could number the dust of the earth, then your descendants also could be numbered. Arise, walk in the land through its length and its width, for I give it to you" (Genesis 13:14–17).

So Abram "moved his tent, and went and dwelt by the terebinth trees of Mamre, which are in Hebron, and built an altar there to the LORD" (verse 18). When Sarah died, Abraham wanted to purchase a fitting burial place. He spoke to the Hittites (the sons of Heth) who owned the land. By that time Abraham was considered a "mighty prince" by these Gentiles. The Hittites offered him the best location, inviting him to choose a burial place. Abraham asked to purchase the cave of Machpelah (see Genesis 23:3–7). The owners wanted to give him the land rather than sell it to him, saying, "My lord, listen to me; the land is worth four hundred shekels of silver. What is that between you and me?" (verse 15).

But Abraham insisted on purchasing the land for four hundred shekels of silver. Hebron became the city of the patriarchs. Abraham and his beloved Sarah, plus Isaac, Rebekah, Jacob, and Leah were all buried there. Centuries later, David ruled in Hebron for seven years before becoming king of Israel. And Abraham's descendants came to be known as Hebrews.

The Fourth Altar in Jerusalem

The first time the words *worship* and *love* are used in Scripture is in the story of Abraham and Isaac. Abraham's fourth altar was built on worship and love. The Lord told Abraham, "Take now your son, your only son Isaac, whom you love, and go to the land of Moriah, and offer him there as a burnt offering on one of the mountains of which I shall tell you" (Genesis 22:2).

Love is one of the most important concepts in Scripture, yet the word is not found until this passage, declaring a father's love for his son. Abraham's love for Isaac is mentioned in an emotionally charged situation.

Abraham rose early the next morning and began his journey, along with two young men and Isaac, to Moriah. They saddled a donkey, traveled for two days, and split wood as they went to prepare for a burnt offering. On the third day Abraham saw their destination ahead. He said to the young men, "Stay here with the donkey; the lad and I will go yonder and worship, and we will come back to you" (verse 5).

This is also the Bible's first use of the word *worship. Worship* means "to bow down," bowing our will to the will of God. Abraham understood this. He was obedient to go, to worship God, and assured the two young men that "we will come back to you." Notice that he used the plural *we.*

God had asked this servant to sacrifice his son, but Abraham believed God would fulfill His promise: "for in Isaac your seed shall be called" (Genesis 21:12). Somehow they both would return. Atop the mountain when Isaac asked, "Where is the lamb for a burnt offering?" his father replied, "My son, God will provide" (Genesis 22:7–8). Abraham built the altar and prepared to sacrifice Isaac, but an angel stopped him. A ram was caught in some nearby bushes, providing the needed sacrifice. Abraham, the loving father, named this altar The-Lord-Will-Provide (verse 14).

The location of this sobering sacrifice and its miraculous conclusion is important. Moriah is the mountain on which Solomon later built the temple. It is in the heart of the city of Jerusalem. (All four of the ancient altars built by Abraham and Jacob were in the mountains of Judea and Samaria in what today is called the West Bank, contested territory between Israel and the Palestinians.)

God's Plan for Everyone

God had a beautiful goal in mind when He promised Abraham, "And in you *all the families of the earth* shall be blessed" (Genesis 12:3). No one is left out of this promised blessing. God manifested His love and grace from the very beginning. We all are His chosen people through the Abrahamic Covenant.

The reach of this promise is confirmed and realized in John's vision in Revelation 7:9–10:

After these things I looked, and behold, a great multitude which no one could
number, of all nations, tribes, peoples, and tongues, standing before the
throne and before the Lamb, clothed with white robes, with palm branches
in their hands, and crying out with a loud voice, saying, "Salvation belongs
to our God who sits on the throne, and to the Lamb!"

There had to be a beginning. God chose one person, Abraham, with whom He
entered into a personal relationship. The great family of God that now reaches every
nation and is offered to all people began with a one-to-one relationship between God
and Abraham.

This was a glorious discovery for me as a Gentile. When I believed in Jesus
Christ as my Lord, Savior, and Messiah, I, too, became a son of the promise, a
spiritual son of Abraham. The apostle Paul explained this:

For they are not all Israel who are of Israel, nor are they all children because
they are the seed of Abraham; but, "In Isaac your seed shall be called." That
is, those who are the children of the flesh, these are not the children of God;
but the children of the promise are counted as the seed. (Romans 9:6–8)

Believers in Jesus Christ are grafted into the Abrahamic Covenant. I have entered into a personal relationship with the God of Abraham, Isaac, and Jacob. And I
have entered into a personal relationship with His people. After my first trip to Israel
I couldn't wait to get back.

Restoring the Glory of the Holy Land

IN ISRAEL A JEWISH CIVIL LEADER TAUGHT ME A NEW perspective on prophecy. This man was a serious student of the Hebrew prophets. In the United States we tend to study prophecy as an intriguing biblical topic. It is ancient and mysterious, and it fascinates us because the prophets were allowed to see the future. God had them record their visions so that we, today, could be aware and ready for what God is preparing to do in the world.

But in Israel the approach to the study of prophecy is different. The words of the prophets are not simply a subject to study, as they might study horticulture or the requirements to construct houses on hilly terrain. For Jews living in Israel today, prophecy is their present as well as their future. For a man such as Ron Nachman, a man who risked his life many times to help establish his people in their God-given homeland, the prophets are describing his life and the lives of his friends and colleagues. What we read as predictions for the future, Nachman and many other Israelis I have come to know read as *their life today.*

Early in September 2001 I had joined other visitors in helping to plant a vineyard near the city of Ariel on the West Bank. Mayor Nachman inspected our work. "This is a prophecy fulfilled," he pronounced while the group brushed soil off their hands. "Today you are fulfilling Jeremiah."

> I will build you up again
>> and you will be rebuilt, O Virgin Israel.
> Again you will take up your tambourines
>> and go out to dance with the joyful.
> Again you will plant vineyards
>> on the hills of Samaria;
> the farmers will plant them
>> and enjoy their fruit.
>
> (Jeremiah 31:4–5, NIV)

The prophet had seen, thousands of years previous to this time, that the barren hills of Samaria would once again flourish. This would be part of the restoration of Israel, and I was with a small group from outside Israel who were blessed to help fulfill the prophecy.

Ron Nachman continued to teach us from the book of Jeremiah: "You shall yet plant vines on the mountains of Samaria.... For there shall be a day when the watchman will cry on Mount Ephraim, 'Arise, and let us go to Zion, to the LORD our God'" (Jeremiah 31:5–6).

"Watchman," he said. "Do you know what this means?" The word *watchman* is translated from the Hebrew word *natsar,* which means "to watch."[1] The original Hebrew for the word *Nazarene* is based on the root word *natsar.* The original followers of Yeshua (Jesus) were known as *Natsarim* (the plural of *Natsari*). Acts 24:5 refers to "the sect of the Nazarenes," the first recorded incident of early Christians being called Nazarenes.

Today, Jews living in the area of Ariel consider Christian pilgrims to be the fulfillment of Jeremiah's prophecy. We were the watchmen planting vines on the mountains of Samaria. We were no longer tourists, nor were we lobbyists or politicians calling for international support of Israel. Mayor Nachman took us to the hills of Samaria because of what the prophets foretold. When the Lord told me it was time to enter into the life and community of Israel, He led me to Ron.

Blueprints of the Temple

I helped plant the Ariel vineyard in early September 2001, just a few months after Benjamin Netanyahu had spoken at a large Calvary Chapel church in Fort Lauderdale, Florida. After leaving Ariel, I was part of a group that had a meeting with the former prime minister in Jerusalem. Mayor Nachman's assistant, Dina Shalit, introduced me. "I'm sure you remember our friends from the events at Calvary Chapel, Fort Lauderdale. Pastor Bentley was there in Fort Lauderdale and had the pleasure of hearing you speak. Ray?" It was time for me to say something.

"We are here to let you know how much we love Israel and that we are with you," I said. "We appreciate you and want to give you this gift as a small reminder that God has good plans in the midst of all that is happening." We were visiting Israel at a particularly volatile time. In light of that, the prime minister thanked me for the gift and chuckled slightly. He said, "God is a good planner."

I tried to convey how much impact his talk at Fort Lauderdale had made across the United States and even around the world. "You bringing that message," I said, "confirms to me that God has a plan for the relationship between Christians and the Jewish people and the state of Israel for such a time as this. Our dream is to build a coalition of churches who may, in a quiet way, have supported you but now will stand more openly."

"Listen," he said soberly, "this is much appreciated and important, especially at this time." Then we saw the prime minister's sense of humor. You need to know that I have grayed over the years, and prior to this meeting the Israeli sun had given me a ruddy complexion. I seem to have resembled a certain US president, and Mr. Netanyahu took notice of this. "But what is Bill Clinton doing here?" he said, and the room erupted in laughter.

Then things got more serious. Mr. Netanyahu left the table and soon returned with a large, framed blueprint. He said, "I just got this from friends of mine. This is the best diagram of the temple and the temple compound, based on historical and archeological evidence. This is actually what the compound really looked like. I got it yesterday and spent two hours just poring over it. It is a reminder of what we are here for."

He pointed out elements of the blueprints, encouraging us to visit the compound, to visit the Western Wall Tunnel, to be near the Holy of Holies. Looking back, now that he is again Israel's prime minister, I realize how significant this is. He is devoted to the temple and to the God of his people.

When I read about him now, as in a *Time* magazine cover story, and realize the scrutiny and pressure he is enduring, I pray for him. As I pray, I remember the relaxed, friendly leader who joked with us and thanked us for our support and friendship. I also believe that God is using him for a very specific purpose: to restore glory to Israel.

To Israel Was Given the Glory

The glory of God, called the Shekhinah, is the beautiful and mysterious manifestation of the invisible God among His people. The apostle Paul wrote,

> I speak the truth in Christ—I am not lying, my conscience confirms it in
> the Holy Spirit—I have great sorrow and unceasing anguish in my heart.
> For I could wish that I myself were cursed and cut off from Christ for the
> sake of my brothers, those of my own race, the people of Israel. Theirs is
> the adoption as sons; *theirs the divine glory,* the covenants, the receiving of
> the law, the temple worship and the promises. Theirs are the patriarchs,
> and from them is traced the human ancestry of Christ, who is God over all,
> forever praised! Amen. (Romans 9:1–5, NIV)

The divine glory belonged first to Israel. The "God of glory," as the Lord is called in Acts 7:2, first manifested His glory in our world at the dawn of creation in a powerful spoken word and burst of light. Adam and Eve knew God in all His glory as He walked with them among the "fiery stones" (Ezekiel 28:14). Noah saw a brilliant flash of God's glory in a multicolored ray of light—the rainbow—a prism of glory, a fractured piece of heaven.

As we have seen, Abraham encountered God's glory when he heard the angel command him to spare Isaac. Abraham must have trembled at the voice of the Lord's messenger that could change death to life in an instant.

Moses witnessed God's glory first in a burning bush, ablaze with a fire that didn't consume, seeing light that wasn't just light. Then he followed the cloud by day and the pillar of fire by night, God's glory that guided the children of Israel to the Promised Land. Later, hiding in a cleft of a rock, Moses was protected just enough to guard his life against the power that no mortal could look upon and survive. He saw just the afterglow of God's glory as the Lord passed by. Moses's face was lit up when he came down from Mount Sinai. Trying to hold on to the glory, Moses covered his face with a veil—as if God could be contained!

Solomon built the temple atop Mount Zion. He dedicated it to the Lord and prayed for His glory to be manifest: "Arise, O LORD God, to Your resting place, You and the ark of Your strength" (2 Chronicles 6:41). He was rewarded with fire that came down from heaven and saw glory fill the temple.

Sadly, the era of Ichabod, which means "the glory of the Lord has departed," cast its shadow over Israel. God reluctantly withdrew His glory in response to His people's unfaithfulness. The temple eventually was destroyed, and the land grew spiritually desolate. Israel soon forgot what it was like to experience the presence of God—until one night hundreds of years later.

While shepherds kept watch over sheep in the hills, the night sky suddenly changed. "The glory of the Lord shone around them," the gospel tells us (Luke 2:9). Heavenly voices heralded the birth of a King. A tiny baby brought the glory of God back to dwell on earth in the Messiah, Jesus. "For in Him dwells all the fullness of the Godhead bodily" (Colossians 2:9). John declared, "The Word became flesh and dwelt among us, and we beheld His glory" (John 1:14).

But God's glory did not stop there. "Christ in you, the hope of glory," the apostle Paul wrote (Colossians 1:27). Jesus called His disciples the branches of the new tree of life: "I am the vine, you are the branches" (John 15:5). He came to baptize us with fire, setting our hearts ablaze with the power of the Holy Spirit. We are now the burning bushes.

After His resurrection, Jesus gathered His followers and "commanded them not to depart from Jerusalem, but to wait for the Promise of the Father, 'which,' He said, 'you have heard from Me; for John truly baptized with water, but you shall be baptized with the Holy Spirit not many days from now'" (Acts 1:4–5). On the day of Pentecost a sound from heaven like a mighty rushing wind brought fire down once again, only this time to rest upon the heads of the early believers. This fire was the glory of God reaching its ultimate destination: the human heart. "And they were all filled with the Holy Spirit" (Acts 2:4).

The disciples began to preach with boldness after they were filled with the Holy Spirit. In their preaching and teaching they witnessed the Holy Spirit touching hearts, minds, and bodies with salvation and healing. God's glory was burning through His bride, the body of Christ. Believers began to stretch out from Jerusalem to the rest of the waiting world.

God still desires to pour out the fullness of His glory, to bring His kingdom to the earth. But there is a divine order the church has forgotten. Once we understand this order, the glory will come. We will see wave after wave of God's glory being poured out for the final and greatest harvest the world has ever seen. Let me explain.

Reconnecting with the Divine Order

For I am not ashamed of the gospel of Christ, for it is the power of God to salvation for everyone who believes, for the Jew first and also for the Greek. For in it the righteousness of God is revealed from faith to faith; as it is written, "The just shall live by faith." (Romans 1:16–17)

"For the Jew first and also for the Greek." This is the divine order. Some think the Jewish people were reached two thousand years ago and that the mandate for "the

Jew first" applied only to the beginning of the church. Yet here we see a principle and much more than that. It is a divine pattern that was established at the beginning of the church. If believers in every generation had reached out in love and grace *to the Jewish people first,* what a different history we might have had!

We know that the original glory of the early church—signs and wonders, miracles, the unity of the body—faded over the years. Occasional bursts of revival fanned into flame in various places. But a study of church history reveals a pattern of not just neglecting God's divine order—"to the Jew first"—but even worse, of allowing anti-Semitic beliefs to take root. Many early church fathers propagated vicious ideas about the Jews. Some even taught the lie that they were cursed for crucifying Jesus. Forgetting that "all have sinned and fall short of the glory of God" (Romans 3:23), the church drifted further away from her first love, Jesus.

This movement is called replacement theology, an erroneous and unbiblical teaching that God's promises to the Jews have been swept aside, that Israel has been replaced by the church. Paul shows us the error of this view:

> And if some of the branches were broken off, and you [Gentiles], being a wild olive tree, were grafted in among them, and with them became a partaker of the root and fatness of the olive tree, do not boast against the branches. But if you do boast, remember that you do not support the root, but the root supports you.
>
> You will say then, "Branches were broken off that I might be grafted in." Well said. Because of unbelief they were broken off, and you stand by faith. Do not be haughty, but fear. For if God did not spare the natural branches, He may not spare you either. (Romans 11:17–21)

Pride caused the natural branches of God's chosen people to be broken off. It had nothing to do with assigning blame for crucifying Christ. Christians need to recognize that the same pride also can break off the grafted-in branches of the Gentiles, that is, the church.

Gentiles who believe in Jesus as Lord and worship the God of Abraham, Isaac, and Jacob are grafted into Israel's olive tree. We are the "wild olive tree" and the other sheep of whom Jesus spoke (John 10:16: "And other sheep I have which are not of this fold; them also I must bring, and they will hear My voice; and there will be one flock and one shepherd").

One flock! Through faith we become connected to the people God chose first as His. Gentile believers are the grafted branches, the other sheep invited to join the flock. The church is not the new branches that have "replaced" the Jews. When the church became disconnected from her Jewish roots, Christians lost the fullness of God's glory. Paul preached in Antioch, "Men of Israel, and you who fear God, listen: The God of this people Israel chose our fathers" (Acts 13:16–17)—a reminder that *God* chose the people of Israel.

All Israel Will Be Saved

God's choosing of Israel was not a response to or a reward for Israel's faithfulness or worthiness. The Jews, just like the rest of humanity, cannot earn His blessing. God does not choose anyone because they deserve to be chosen (see Romans 9:16). Daniel Gruber has pointed out: "God chose the smallest, least powerful, most despised people, so that He could show His love and His power, and bring down the big, mighty, and esteemed."[2]

Paul pronounced a future salvation so sweeping that "all Israel will be saved."

For I do not desire, brethren, that you should be ignorant of this mystery, lest you should be wise in your own opinion, that blindness in part has happened to Israel until the fullness of the Gentiles has come in. And so all Israel will be saved, as it is written:

"The Deliverer will come out of Zion,
And He will turn away ungodliness from Jacob;
For this is My covenant with them,
When I take away their sins." (Romans 11:25–27)

Paul then declares an astounding truth too often quoted out of context: "For the gifts and calling of God are irrevocable" (Romans 11:29). He is referring here to the Jewish people. This verse usually is applied to anything and everyone *except* the Jews. But let's take a more careful look. Paul is referring to the gifts and calling God gave to His chosen people: "For God has committed them all to disobedience, that He might have mercy on all. Oh, the depth of the riches both of the wisdom and knowledge of God! How unsearchable are His judgments and His ways past finding out!" (Romans 11:32–33).

The promises God made to Abraham, Isaac, and Jacob are forever. If He fails to keep those promises, what assurance do Christians have that He will keep His promises to us?

The good news is that God is keeping His eternal covenant with the Jewish people, and He is doing it in full view of the entire world. We can be confident that He will keep all the promises He has made. Our heavenly Father is long-suffering and patient. He is working in our hearts to bring the church back to her roots and to our unique role in loving the Jews through practical, tangible, and spiritual means. This is how we can follow the divine order. This will reconnect us to God's glory. This will empower us to be His bride, fulfilling the Great Commission for such a time as this.

PART 2

How Prophecy Is
Being Revealed Today

A Personal Introduction
to an Unlikely Prophet

IN 1998 ROBERT MAWIRE STOOD BEFORE PRIME
Minister Benjamin Netanyahu of Israel. Mawire, an African Christian, had traveled
from the United States to Jerusalem to deliver a message from God. He knew the
Lord wanted him to pass this message on to the prime minister: "The day you negotiate land for peace, your government will collapse."

Mr. Netanyahu laughed quietly. Looking Robert in the eye, he said, "Have you
not read in your Bible that we stone our prophets in this country?" He dismissed
Mawire's words as just another loony statement from a Christian suffering the "Jerusalem Syndrome" delusion. That is a phenomenon where would-be messiahs and
other misguided people become intoxicated by the Holy City and act mentally dis-
turbed.[1] Shortly afterward, in October 1998, a marathon meeting with Netanyahu
and Palestinian Authority president Yasir Arafat was held. Mediated by President
Bill Clinton, the session resulted in a "breakthrough land-for-peace deal in the West
Bank."[2]

By July 1999 Netanyahu was out of office, his government having collapsed. In
2001 Robert Mawire again met with the former prime minister; this time the two
men were friends. The prophet from Africa had another word from the Lord: "Be

strong and of good courage. God is not done with you. You will be prime minister again at a critical time in history. Don't ever negotiate land for peace again."

Netanyahu became prime minister again in 2009. At this writing he is engaged in a struggle to navigate the never-ending peace negotiations. I wonder how often the words of this unlikely prophet intrude upon his thoughts and decisions.

There are Christians who resist the idea that God uses special messengers today in a way similar to the ancient prophets. I won't argue the point. I will simply let Robert Mawire tell his story.

"I was cursed before I was born! Cursed to be a struggling nothing." That is Robert Mawire's description of his early life. "I was supposed to be special. They told me I would carry on the work of my father. But I hated it. It was a terrible fate. I hated God for choosing me to become a struggling nothing." Then he laughed and slapped his hands together. Mawire laughs hard and often.

The things that happen to this man don't happen to ordinary people. Yet he explains his life simply as a believer who does nothing more than live in the grace of God. When he tells his story, he never casts himself as anything beyond ordinary.

"Mzungu," he intones. "Do you know this word? It means 'white man,' like you."

"This mzungu named John G. Lake walked through the hotel in Johannesburg, South Africa, where my father was a chef. People started screaming and yelling [at the sight of Lake]. People were healed, falling to their knees and confessing their sins. John G. Lake would just walk through, and people would crawl to him, crying. John G. Lake would hug them or hold their hands and tell them it was Jesus who loved them and wanted to heal and forgive them."

Robert's father heard the commotion and left the kitchen to ask the white man, "What's happening here?" And Lake told him it was Jesus.

"My father was a Methodist deacon in his church, but he had never seen God move like this!" Robert says. "It was as if Jesus had come to town. My father wanted to know more." As John Lake discipled and trained Mawire's father, his father vowed that if more people like Lake would come, he would quit his job and move back to his native Rhodesia (now Zimbabwe), where he would start a mission center. Robert was born in Rhodesia, the sixth child of his family, but the first born at the new Rufaro Mission Compound.

"They tell me that while my mom was pregnant, the missionaries had a prophecy for my parents—that this baby would be named Robert, and he would carry on the work they had begun. I grew up thinking I was special. The missionaries would see me and say, 'That's the boy. The one who will finish the work.'

"But when I got to high school and told the teachers I was going to be a preacher, every kid laughed. Suddenly I wasn't special. I was cursed!" Anger and embarrassment drove Mawire away from the church and straight into Robert Mugabe's Communist Party.

"I became a preacher after all. I spoke everywhere, telling people, 'The greatest enemy of our people right now is my dad. My dad tells people not to worry about what you will eat or how you will live, and that if you follow the missionaries, when you die, you will go to heaven.'

"I decided we needed to make heaven now," he continues. "I told them the Bible was riddled with errors.... I became very sophisticated in my own mind, telling whoever would listen that the Bible is the white man's tool and that my dad was the real problem. [But in truth] I was the tool being used by the communists."

He folds his hands, leans forward, and whispers, "I wanted power.

"You see," his voice rising, "before the colonization [of Rhodesia] my family was a royal family. They were rulers, kings, and queens. We once ruled; now we are ruled. Now we follow missionaries. I didn't want to be told what to do. I wanted to be president. That's what I thought I was born to do. I thought I could find power by fighting the missionaries and my parents. I was so lost."

When he is asked how his parents handled all this, the smile comes back.

"Oh, my mom and dad, Ernest and Tabitha Mawire, the greatest couple, married eighty years. Every morning at 4 a.m. while I was growing up, they were singing and praying. Every single morning. I was so irritated! 'Why,' I would ask them, 'do you have to do that when we're trying to sleep?'"

His parents had all the missionaries praying for their son. "Then one day while I was out giving my stupid speech about the Bible being full of errors, a young man challenged me to show him the errors. I had a big ego. I knew I could prove it, so I decided to find those errors. My ego kept reading and reading, but I wasn't seeing errors or contradictions. I was seeing God in story after story, verse after verse.

"Then I read John 1:12—'But as many as received Him, to them He gave the right to become children of God, to those who believe in His name'—and I had a powerful encounter with the Jesus of the Bible. Not a historical, theological Jesus, but a radical, real encounter that opened my eyes. I knew my father was not deceived; it had been me."

Mawire, converted after encountering Jesus, began sharing his testimony. "The grace of God and the prayers of the missionaries brought me back. But I still didn't want to be a preacher." Maybe not, but his life was in danger.

The communists did more than object to the change in his public speeches. They tried to kill him. "They would bring my friends to me with their ears and lips chopped off and say, 'This is what we are going to do to you and your family.' They killed my friends. They put rubber tires around their necks and burned them. We lived for a month with these thugs surrounding our house." He explains that his family went to bed every night hoping and praying they wouldn't be torched, kidnapped, tortured, or murdered.

"Finally," Mawire says, "I asked one of my former colleagues [among the communists], 'What are you waiting for?' And he told me they knew my father had connections. 'Connections!' I yelled at him. 'What do you mean?' And he told me, 'All the soldiers you hired to protect your compound.'

"Ha!" Robert exclaims. "We had no soldiers. No one protected us. But they saw an army surrounding us. God had sent *His* army, His angels. And they had no idea we were just sitting there, protected only by prayer."

One morning the reluctant preacher sat at the back of a church, mentally making fun of the accent of a visiting Dutch preacher. Mawire was startled when the preacher called him out by name. Mawire stood up, and the man said God had something for him to do, something Robert had written about in his journal.

"I gave up then," Robert says with a smile. "God had specifically answered the prayer I had written down in my journal. No one else knew about it, and here I was being publicly called!"

His life was still in constant danger, so Mawire's family agreed that Robert needed to leave Africa—eventually leading to his deep involvement with Israel. At the time he was co-pastor of a small church in Fort Worth, Texas. "I was the black pastor in an all-white church with not enough to do." That changed after a believer prophesied that Robert would help the Jews.

"I thought the guy was crazy," he says. "But every time I went to sleep I would dream about what he said. I loved to study prophecy, and to study prophecy is to study Israel and the God of Abraham, Isaac, and Jacob. I began to dream even more. God spoke to me again and again and told me I was to go see Benjamin Netanyahu, the prime minister of Israel, and tell him, 'You cannot negotiate land for peace or your government will collapse.'... Every time I prayed, God spoke those words to me."

But how would an African pastor ministering in Texas ever get an audience with Israel's prime minister? The answer is, in a roundabout way.

Robert continues: "The Lord told me to go to Dallas and a man would put his hand on my shoulder and tell me, 'It's your time to go speak to Benjamin Netanyahu.'" Robert went to Dallas after asking God to have someone tell him where in Dallas he could find this man. At a businessmen's meeting he encountered a man who had hurt his back. Just as Robert stretched his arm toward him, the man stopped him and said, "Man of God, before you pray, the answer to your prayer about where in Dallas something is supposed to happen is the Grand Kempinski Hotel."

Sure enough, the following Thursday at the Grand Kempinski, where Robert had been invited to speak, a gentleman put his hand on Robert's shoulder and said, "Your time to speak to Benjamin Netanyahu has come."

"How do you know?" Robert asked. The man responded, "The Lord has told me. Give me your phone number, and I will put you in touch with people."

Ron Nachman, who later became my close friend, called Robert and then flew to Texas from Israel. Robert poured out his passion for Israel, took Nachman through the Scriptures and his study of prophecy, and discussed God's covenant with His people. He told Nachman that he had a message from God for the prime minister. When Robert finished, the mayor of Ariel slapped the table. "Okay," he said. "I will go back and tell Benjamin Netanyahu that there is a man from God with a word for him."

Weeks later Robert delivered his message to the prime minister in Israel, in the presence of several cabinet members, including the future Prime Minister Ariel Sharon. How did he find himself laughing with the prime minister, delivering such a powerful message, and beginning what would become a friendly and deeply spiritual relationship?

"I don't know," said Mawire. "I am a nobody in this world, but God is an awesome, awesome, awesome God."

An Ancient Gentile Points the Way

"JEW AND GENTILE ARE TWO WORLDS," WROTE Jewish novelist Maurice Samuels. "Between you Gentiles and us Jews there lies an unbridgeable gulf.... There are two life forces in the world: Jewish and Gentile.... I do not believe that this primal difference between Gentile and Jew is reconcilable."[1]

"An unbridgeable gulf" is the phrase Samuels used to describe the distance between the Jewish people and the rest of the world, meaning the Gentiles. I long to help build the bridge that will join us. It is time for the church to rediscover her Hebrew roots and for believers in Jesus to help build the bridge. Or perhaps we are supposed to be the bridge.

What We Are Missing

Just when I was wrestling with how to come to a deeper understanding of my Jewish friends, I met a remarkable teacher who changed the way I study the Bible. This man, who is referred to by some as Blood Moon Biltz (see the description of his research into blood moons in chapter 20), teaches the Bible from the perspective of the original language and Scripture's Hebrew roots.

"Anti-Semitism and replacement theology have crippled our understanding of God and the covenant He made with His people, the Jews," Mark Biltz said to me during one of our many conversations. He never fails to surprise me with new twists on familiar scriptures.

"Do you know what the first letter of the Hebrew alphabet means?" asked this pastor with a Jewish ancestry and a zeal for Hebrew tradition. (He is helping to build the bridge between Jews and Gentiles.) He explained that the first letter of the Hebrew alphabet is *aleph,* and it has a three-part construction. In the exalted position as the head of the alphabet, aleph is not just the equivalent of the letter *A.* Jewish theologians look at it as the lord and master of all letters, made in the image of God. Each letter is assigned a numeric value, so aleph is one.

When you break the letter down into its three parts, you find some fascinating things. Aleph (א) is made up of two *yods* (י) separated by a slanted *vav* (ו). Aleph, symbolic of God, is three-in-one.[2]

A rich culture is hiding in plain sight in the Hebrew language. For another example, we'll look at a familiar story that takes on a much deeper meaning when it is read in light of its Jewish origin.

What's in a Name?

Centuries after Abraham lived, Israel entered a dark time when the judges ruled the land and the people rebelled against God. "There was no king in Israel; everyone did what was right in his own eyes," wrote the prophet Samuel, describing one of the lowest points in Israel's history (Judges 17:6). It was a time of moral drifting, spiritual confusion, division, cruelty, and apostasy.[3]

Famine drove many Hebrews out of Israel and into foreign lands. One of those Jewish men ended up in Moab, where he met and fell in love with Ruth, deciding to take her as his wife. Ruth was a Gentile, and her story is told in one of the most beloved books in the Old Testament. The mood of this story, as well as its plot line, are revealed in the names of the characters. Look at this cast:

- Elimelech: Naomi's Hebrew husband and Ruth's father-in-law. He emigrated from Bethlehem in Israel to Moab to escape the famine. His name means "my God is king."

- Naomi: Elimelech's wife. Her name means "pleasant," "gracious one," or "my delight." She later changed her name to Mara, which means "bitter."
- Mahlon and Chilion: sons of Elimelech and Naomi. They must have been born in poor health; their names mean "sickly" and "weak." Ruth was married to Mahlon.
- Ruth: a native of Moab and thus a Gentile. Her name means "friend."
- Orpah: Ruth's sister-in-law. Orpah married Chilion. Her name means "gazelle" or "mane," from the root word for "back of the neck."
- Boaz: a Hebrew who remained in Israel. He was Naomi's relative who welcomed Ruth and Naomi home after they suffered a series of setbacks. Boaz is the biblical illustration of a kinsman redeemer. He rescued Ruth and Naomi, and his name means "he comes in strength."
- Obed: son of Ruth and Boaz, father of Jesse, who became the father of King David. His name means "servant."

Elimelech left Bethlehem and took his family to Moab. There he died, leaving Naomi in a foreign land where widows were ignored or, worse, preyed upon. Her two sons married Moabite women, giving her two daughters-in-law: Orpah and Ruth. Naomi could envision a future of grandchildren—until her sons died.

As Naomi's sorrow turned to bitterness and anger, she decided to return to her people. With that decision made, she told her daughters-in-law to remain with their own people in Moab. "Go, return each to her mother's house…," she urged, "for it grieves me very much for your sakes that the hand of the LORD has gone out against me!" (Ruth 1:8, 13). The women wept as Orpah kissed Naomi and turned away. But Ruth refused to leave Naomi.

Naomi persisted. "Look, your sister-in-law has gone back to her people and her gods" (verse 15). But Ruth refused, saying: "Entreat me not to leave you, or to turn back from following after you; for wherever you go, I will go; and wherever you lodge, I will lodge; your people shall be my people, and your God, my God. Where you die, I will die, and there will I be buried. The LORD do so to me, and more also, if anything but death parts you and me" (verses 16–17).

Naomi couldn't fight Ruth's determination. Together they trudged back to Bethlehem, arriving at Naomi's home at the beginning of the barley harvest. Excited greetings rang out all over the city. But when the women called out her name, Naomi cried back, "Do not call me Naomi; call me Mara, for the Almighty has dealt very bitterly with me. I went out full, and the LORD has brought me home again empty. Why do you call me Naomi, since the LORD has testified against me, and the Almighty has afflicted me?" (verses 20–21). Her sorrow and discouragement threatened to change her identity and personality. But an ancient law and a clever plan were about to turn things around.

The Law of Gleaning

Ruth's devotion to Naomi meant she was determined to provide for her mother-in-law. Aware of the law that commanded farmers to leave grain behind for the poor to gather (see Leviticus 19:9–10), Ruth asked Naomi's permission to go to the fields. "Go, my daughter," Naomi answered (Ruth 2:2). Ruth ended up in a field belonging to Boaz, a relative of Elimelech. Mere coincidence? Rabbis say that *coincidence* is not a kosher word.

As Boaz rode through his fields, he was attracted to a young woman gathering the grain that had been left behind. His overseer told him the woman was the Moabite who had arrived with Naomi (see verses 6–7). Boaz went to Ruth. "Do not go to glean in another field, nor go from here, but stay close by my young women" (verse 8). Soon he was inviting her to eat with him, offering her protection, and instructing the other workers, "Let her gather grain right among the sheaves without stopping her. And pull out some heads of barley from the bundles and drop them on purpose for her" (verses 15–16, NLT).

When Ruth came home laden with grain, Naomi said of Boaz: "Blessed be he of the LORD!... This man is a relation of ours, one of our close relatives" (verse 20).

Ruth worked in Boaz's fields until the end of the barley and wheat harvests, and Naomi developed a plan to secure a future for both of them. One evening, knowing that Boaz would be winnowing barley on the threshing floor, Naomi told Ruth to bathe and perfume herself and dress in her nicest garment. Ruth did this, and Naomi sent her to the threshing floor. She instructed Ruth to wait until after Boaz finished eating and drinking and then to go to the place where he would be sleeping. There, Ruth was to lift up his blanket and lie at his feet. Ruth did all this.

At midnight Boaz awoke, startled to see a young woman at his feet. Ruth told him, "Spread the corner of your covering over me, for you are my family redeemer" (Ruth 3:9, NLT).

Boaz was enthusiastic in his response: "You have shown more kindness at the end than at the beginning, in that you did not go after young men, whether poor or rich. And now, my daughter, do not fear. I will do for you all that you request" (verses 10–11). He had fallen in love with Ruth and immediately took care of the legal process that allowed him to become her kinsman redeemer.

Boaz married Ruth, and she gave him a son, Obed, the grandfather of King David. Eventually, this anointed and respected genealogy birthed Yeshua, the Messiah.

A Love Story

What role do Gentiles play in the historic drama that began with Abraham, Ishmael, Isaac, and Jacob? Are we persecutors of the Jews, judges, spectators, or sympathizers? What kind of relationship can Christians build with the Jewish people? Ruth's story answers many of these questions. It is an allegory of the relationship between the church and the Jewish people. Her story exemplifies the heart of God because it is a love story.

As we read about Ruth's life, we are impressed by her love for Naomi and for Boaz and vice versa. This is a picture of the love between God and His people as He blesses the Jewish nation through a Gentile. It is the story of God's great love for the world, and each character represents a greater truth.

- Elimelech and his family represent the nation of Israel.
- Naomi depicts the Jewish people scattered in exile.

- Boaz represents the faithful Jewish remnant that remained in the land.
- Ruth personifies the Gentiles.

Ruth belonged to a cursed people, the Moabites, who specifically were forbidden to enter into the assembly of the Lord (see Deuteronomy 23:3). Since she was from a pagan, idol-worshiping culture, her conversion and choice to embrace the God of Abraham make her a courageous and endearing historical figure. Some of the greatest love stories take place in difficult, war-torn times. Ruth's story is no exception.

At the Crossroads

The era of the judges was a difficult time in Israel. Widespread famine affected even Bethlehem, the "house of bread." Elimelech chose to run away. I don't want to be too hard on him; he was trying to provide for his family. And remember that Abraham did the same thing when he fled to Egypt to find food for his family. But the deaths of Elimelech and his sons left three women mourning, alone, and highly vulnerable in Moab.

But when Naomi returned home with Ruth, they found Boaz and his family prospering. I believe God turned this tragedy into something good for Israel and the world.

Remember, Ruth's name means "friend" or "companion." Orpah's name comes from a word meaning "the back of the neck" or "to turn the neck." In the end Ruth clung to Naomi; Orpah turned away.

Naomi foreshadows the Jews returning to their homeland in the twentieth century. Her sorrow foreshadows the terrible loss of men and women, sons and daughters during the Holocaust in addition to the centuries of persecution that preceded Nazi Germany's attempted extermination of the Jewish race. After her husband and sons died in Moab, Naomi returned to Bethlehem. She had nowhere else to go. Today, Jews from around the world ask the same question: "Where can we go?" And, like Naomi, they are returning to Israel.

The Gentiles in this story—Orpah and Ruth—represent two responses to the Jewish people: those who turn their backs on the nation of Israel and those who embrace the Jews and enter into the story of their return. At the fork in the road, Ruth made a choice to enter the story. Clutching Naomi's garment, she said, "I am holding on to you, to your God, and to the promises God has given you and your precious people." She fell in love with the God of Abraham, Isaac, and Jacob.

This hallmark conversion and Ruth's famous words often are cited in Jewish literature as an example of a true, heartfelt conversion to the Jewish faith.[4] Naomi also was blessed in the process. Her life was restored by the love of a Gentile. I can picture the older woman smiling as she held Obed, the son of Ruth, cherishing the warmth and healing of his little life. Obed would be the grandfather of Israel's greatest king and an ancestor of the Messiah, the Savior of the world.

Bridge Building

God's people lived outside the Promised Land for a very long time, and now they are being called home. While in exile many Jews lost their faith. And now, like Naomi, their journey back to Israel is burdened by bitterness and anger. They have little reason to trust the shaky bridge that people like me are attempting to build. They are suspicious of the friendship being extended by Gentiles, especially those who profess belief in Jesus. The "unbridgeable gulf" we read about earlier is too real.

But the story of Ruth reinforces my conviction that Israel is not supposed to return alone to the land. God is inviting the church to travel with His chosen people, to bless Naomi's descendants, to build the bridge.

When you think about building the bridge, think of the first letter of the Hebrew alphabet: aleph. Mark, my friend and teacher, pointed out, "Aleph is what links heaven and earth—just like Jacob's ladder." Jacob, fleeing across the desert from his brother Esau, slept one night on a stone pillow. He dreamed that "a ladder was set up on the earth, and its top reached to heaven; and there the angels of God were ascending and descending on it" (Genesis 28:12).

Centuries later, Jesus said to His disciples, "You shall see heaven open, and the angels of God ascending and descending upon the Son of Man" (John 1:51). My friend Mark likes to say, "The aleph is the bridge, and who is the aleph? Yeshua the

Messiah." Jesus is the bridge that will draw His people and His church together. And we, the body of the Messiah, are the building pieces, spanning that wide, deep chasm with love and compassion. One day the hearts of the Gentiles will be joined to the hearts and souls of the chosen people.

I had asked God to keep opening doors, to draw me deeper into His land and her people. He reminded me that other descendants of Abraham live in the Promised Land. Some never left, and they often feel slighted and hurt by people like me. Many of them are my brothers and sisters, yearning for a relationship and acknowledgment of the deep bond we share through the blood of our Savior.

In my zeal to get to know the Jews, I almost ignored the children of Abraham's other son, Ishmael.

Learning from the Descendants of Ishmael

AT THE 1956 FUNERAL OF A YOUNG FARMER IN Kibbutz Nahal-Oz in Israel, military leader and Israeli hero Moshe Dayan expressed empathy and a sensitivity to the feelings of Arabs. His statement surprised many of his followers. "Let us not fling accusations at the murderers. What cause have we to complain about their fierce hatred to us? For eight years now, they sit in their refugee camps in Gaza, and before their eyes we turn into our homestead the land and villages in which they and their forefathers have lived."[1]

At first I was surprised—and challenged—to read his words. The church I pastor in San Diego holds four services every weekend. While the congregation gathers inside, a man stands outside. Every weekend he holds a vigil in defense of Palestinians whom he believes are harmed by my church's support of Israel. His vigil is respectful, peaceful, and legal. One of the signs he holds reads "Palestinians need love too."

He sent me a letter stating that people who attend churches such as Maranatha Chapel "have not fully reflected on the pain and suffering that their brand of Christianity causes millions of Palestinian men, women and children every day." I agree with his statement. I am aware that in our zeal to support Israel and the Jewish people we run the risk of missing the whole story. When God made it clear that Abraham's son Isaac was the son of promise, the Lord also made a far-reaching promise to Ishmael, the son whom Abraham banished to the desert. If we limit our interest in the Middle East just to Jews living in Israel, we are turning our backs on millions of people who also descend from Abraham and his son Ishmael.

How could Ishmael not be bitter about the treatment he received? How could he not resent Isaac? Other than a brief reconciliation at Abraham's death, the two brothers and their descendants perpetuated their animosity into our century and into our lives. Christians need to guard against an overly narrow, limited perspective regarding Israel. God restored the Jews to their homeland, and we rejoice in that. But God has not forgotten the Gentiles who descended from Abraham. And we need to be aware of what they bring to our understanding of Scripture. Don't forget Ruth, a woman from the pagan Moabites who is named with honor in the genealogy of Jesus, the Messiah.

I want to introduce you to three of my friends. They also are believers in Jesus, and they see the ongoing Mideast conflict differently than some of my Jewish friends. Because of these men, I think often of Ishmael being sent away by his father.

Botrus Mansour: An Arab, Israeli, Palestinian Christian

Botrus Mansour is the general director of one of the most prestigious schools in Israel. He serves as a bridge between Christians and the Muslim world. "One day," he told me, "I asked, 'What would Jesus want an Arab, Israeli, Palestinian, evangelical Christian raised by Greek Orthodox and Catholic parents and living in His hometown, Nazareth, to do?'"

Botrus helped create the Nazareth Village, a replica of the village where Jesus grew up. I was touring this village when I met him. He is kind, intelligent, handsome, and soft-spoken. He looks very much like the academic he is. He is a lawyer as well as an educator, and he speaks fluent Hebrew.

Because he represents an unusual combination of ethnicity and faith, he is a minority among Christians (he is an evangelical) and among Muslim Arabs (he is Christian). To further complicate things, he is a minority Arab living among Jewish Israelis. He is an Israeli citizen but also a Palestinian.

He is an Arab Christian who points out that Arabs were present in Jerusalem on the day of Pentecost (see Acts 2). Arabs accepted the new faith from the beginning, and Arab Christian tribes thrived in the Middle East from the earliest days of Christianity. "Arab Christians," he says, "have been living in the Middle East among Muslims and Jews as a struggling minority of second-class citizens for generations."

I found Botrus and his colleagues to be friendly and obviously filled with the Holy Spirit. But I also could feel the tension between Arab Christians and Jews.

Botrus's father, a renowned journalist, came from the village of Jish, at the foot of Israel's Mount Meron. His mother's father was a police officer in Cana, near Galilee. His mother has the distinction of being the first woman from Cana to earn a high school diploma—from the school where she would later teach and where Botrus now serves as general director.

His parents combined their Greek Orthodox and Catholic backgrounds to raise Botrus and his siblings in a church environment. He recalls, "I came to faith at a young age, having gone forward at a revival meeting."

He made another commitment later, while in high school, under the influence of George Laty, who became a beloved mentor. Botrus embraced the evangelical Baptist tradition in spite of his background. He went on to study at the Hebrew University of Jerusalem, working in law offices where he became deeply involved in human rights issues. Through his work and his commitment to make a difference, he reaches into many worlds. "People assume I am Muslim," he says. "They forget there were Arabs before Islam."

He speaks softly, but his emotions at times are intense. "As a believer, I want to walk in the will of God. But at the same time my earthly affiliations and identities cause me to push in different directions, especially in this land of conflict."

He decries the gap between the small community of evangelical believers in Israel, people like himself, and the Western evangelical church. "As an evangelical living in Israel, I don't experience a bond with evangelicals from abroad. Distance and different cultures are part of the reason. But when I watch Christian television or meet American evangelicals, I feel like we should be connected; we have the same faith. But I don't feel like part of the family; the relationship is strained, full of misunderstanding. Their support for the Jews is unconditional, but Palestinian

Christians are almost an embarrassment [to them]. I love Israel. I am Israeli too. We are your brothers and sisters in Jesus living in His hometown.

"Yet," he says, "the tour bus rolls right by us. We are forgotten."

Botrus's longing for acknowledgment from the Western church shook me. "Jesus emphasized the spiritual bond and relationship of the family of God," he began. "There's a story in Arabic about two brothers who quarrel over land, water, issues of property. They fight and carry on, but ultimately they reconcile—because at the end of the day, their blood relationship holds them together.

"The blood of Jesus is not something we dispute. The blood He shed gives salvation to the world. His blood is supposed to forge in us a special bond, one church around the world with many nationalities. His blood makes us closer and is more important than being born into a family—which is important, but not as important as the family of God."

A Telling Perspective on Israel's Rebirth

Western Christians who love Israel view the year 1948 as a miraculous turning point. It was the year when Palestine was designated, once again, as the Jewish homeland. Jews began to return after almost two millenniums. The modern state of Israel was born.

Then I learned how Botrus and his family regard the historic events of Israel. He refers to the "war of 1948" as a "difficult time." His father, who was in junior high school at the time, had been sent to Lebanon to finish his schooling. But he wanted to get home when the war broke out, so he sneaked across the border and into the newly formed state of Israel.

"In Israel," Botrus says, "you're okay as an Arab. A second-class citizen and marginalized, but okay." He acknowledged, "We do live better in Israel than in other Arab countries, but there's still a problem. One cannot ignore the suffering Palestinians have endured since hundreds of thousands became refugees in 1948."

Or the discrimination his own family has endured. His sister, Samar, was born in Israel. She is a committed Christian who married a Jordanian pastor. She resigned her job in the Israeli Ministry of Health and moved to Amman, Jordan, with her husband. When her mother became seriously ill, the couple decided to move to Nazareth so Samar could help with her mother's care.

"Israel refused my brother-in-law's request to live in Nazareth," said Botrus. "In Israel's eyes, an Arab is an Arab...never mind that my sister, born in Israel with ancestors that go back for centuries, worked for the Ministry of Health nor that our father was a journalist in the prestigious Israeli newspaper *Haaretz*. My grandfather Botrus, born in 1898 in a small village in the north of Israel, farmed and built [a life] there. His father lived there before him. We have been in the land all these years."

Botrus acted as his brother-in-law's lawyer, filing lawsuits with the Supreme Court. Months later they won a "permit of entrance." Knowing how hard the Israeli government works to welcome Jews to resettle in Israel and to become citizens, Botrus admits, "The case left a bitter taste in our mouths."

An Arab's View of the Holocaust

"No words can adequately describe the...disgust every person should feel toward such awful, satanic activities," Botrus wrote of the Holocaust. "Zionism wanted to establish a home for the Jews who had suffered from persecution...which peaked with the Holocaust.... This dreadful deed was the underpinning of the establishment of the state of Israel."[2]

"The Jews were a people without a land," he said somberly, "but they came to a land with people, thriving communities. Of course the inevitable clash came, and the Palestinians lost. More than four hundred villages were evacuated, and people became refugees.... That's what happened from my point of view." He stopped and shrugged. "But I am trying to be fair."

Finally I asked Botrus how Jesus answered his original question: What would Jesus want an Arab Israeli Palestinian evangelical Christian raised by Greek Orthodox and Catholic parents living in His hometown to do?

"The Lord has prepared me to minister for Him in His hometown in a unique way," he said. Working through the Nazareth Baptist School, Botrus and his colleagues are a bridge that crosses another seemingly unbridgeable gulf: linking the Christian, Muslim, and Jewish worlds. The student population of the school is more than 20 percent Muslim. Botrus's quiet, diplomatic demeanor has navigated dangerous conflicts between powerful Muslim families who were determined to send their kids to the finest school in Israel—sometimes at great risk to Botrus and his team. He and his teachers have planted seeds of the gospel in children from Catholic, Baptist, Protestant, Greek Orthodox, and Muslim backgrounds. Many go on to influence their communities as teachers, lawyers, doctors, ministers, and business people.

"My heavenly identity is most important," Botrus said. "I want to love my neighbor, not put on masks, be what the Lord wants me to be." To American Christians he says, "We're your brothers and sisters here. We are a small minority, we have challenges, but please remember that we exist. We are the living stones among the ancient stones in this small hometown of our Lord Jesus Christ. It would be easier to move to America, where we won't feel excluded. But we know we are called to be here and to work for transformative change in the land of our Savior."

While Botrus diligently works for his convictions through the law and education, my next friend fought with hatred precisely aimed through the scope of a sniper's rifle.

A Friend Asks, "How Did I Not Die?"

Tass Saada once relished killing Jews and Christians. He was a sniper for the Palestinian Liberation Organization (PLO). In those years he was a fiery, violent radical who revered Yasir Arafat as a hero and thought of himself as the Rambo of the PLO. Today, Tass is a committed Christian, and he is forceful in his convictions. He slapped the tabletop and vehemently declared, "He is the God of Abraham, Isaac, *Ishmael,* and Jacob!" He is strong in his opinions and passionate about reconciliation between Arabs and Jews.

Tass's family called the events of 1948 *al-Nakba,* meaning "the catastrophe." After the Arab governments ordered his family to leave their home, they spent three years in a tent in the dismal refugee camps of Gaza, where Tass was born in 1951. To escape refugee life, they moved to Saudi Arabia, where he grew up Muslim and was taught to hate the Jews. Seeds of his bitterness sank deep into his psyche.

In 1967 I was an eleven-year-old American boy intrigued by Bible prophecy and the headlines heralding the Six-Day War. But Tass, only a few years older than I, watched the war from the heart of the Arab world. For him, it was not just headlines. The Israeli victory left him seething with anger and Arab pride.

"We had lost," he cried. "What a terrible embarrassment! The resentment I had sustained all my life took a quantum leap."[3]

"My father was one of the biggest donors for Fatah," Tass explained. So it was not surprising when an emerging charismatic leader of this faction of the PLO was a frequent dinner guest at the Saada home. "I sat next to him [Arafat] because he was my hero. I listened, mesmerized. He was our leader."

The 1967 Six-Day War was the catalyst. Tass left home and joined the PLO against his father's wishes. He became a Fatah fighter, a trained sniper, and Arafat's personal driver. He was teamed with the first Palestinian suicide bombers. They jumped off roofs under which Tass fired on military personnel and civilians alike. He assassinated, bombed, and fought hand to hand. "We were ready to die," he said.

"When I came to the Lord, I had flashbacks. I remember exact situations where I know I should have died, where I ask, 'How did I not die?'"

Once, sitting on a bridge with two other fighters, chatting quietly so as not to be heard by Israelis across the river, Tass heard Israeli artillery let loose. "My two guys exploded. I was covered in flesh and blood and thought I had been hit too.… I drove to a clinic and discovered I had only a scratch.

"Oh, my head got so big after that!… I thought I was Rambo, indestructible. I took to wearing chain bullets and carried a Victory AK47. Whatever I didn't like, I shot."

Hearing his story, I tried to picture the young, radical Tass with automatic rifles slung across his scarred fighter's body. This solid, grandfatherly-looking man, with his soft, Saudi accent; dark, intense eyes; and graying fringe around his balding pate, still exuded strength and purpose. Today he fights just as fiercely, but now for peace.

"Arafat was a fox," he said, "but misunderstood. When we fought alongside him, he inspired us to sacrifice. You know, he didn't need to do this. The man was very wealthy, friends with the prince of Kuwait, had an engineering degree and business. He gave all his money and his life for a cause he believed right. The media gave him a dark history.

"I visited him before he died. After thirty-four years, when I walked in the door, he got up, kissed me on both cheeks, took my hand and set my chair close to him. He never asked me why I had converted [to Christianity], but he knew about my work. He began bragging to me about how he took care of Christians. He married a Catholic woman, you know. Why? He wanted the world to know that he doesn't discriminate. He wanted a relationship with the church."

His fifteen-minute visit with the PLO leader turned into an hour, then dinner, during which Tass shared much of his life and relationship with the Lord. Five months later Arafat died.

Finding Reconciliation

Tass Saada's journey took him to the United States, where he met his wife, Karen. He acquired an education and one day found himself on his knees, bathed in a miraculous light and surrendering his life to Jesus. Everything changed—especially when Tass realized he was praying for Israel and asking God to bless her people. "I had never wished a good thing for Jews my entire life."

A ministry of reconciliation grew from his new faith, a vision to reconcile Arabs and Jews through the gospel of Jesus. "There are no other answers for peace in the Middle East," he said.

He loves to correct the misconceptions that most Christians hold about Arabs, dating back to Abraham and Ishmael. "Nothing negative was ever said about Hagar and Ishmael in the writings of the rabbis," he explains. "Look at Genesis 16." Then he read, " 'Sarai...took Hagar her maid, the Egyptian, and gave her to her husband Abram to be his wife.' Wife, not concubine!" he exclaimed. "That elevates the status of Hagar and Ishmael considerably."

The rabbis taught that Hagar was an Egyptian princess given to Sarai. "And think of the rejection Ishmael felt! Almost seventeen years old, sent out into the desert by his father. I used to be so mad at Abraham—*what a cheapskate,* I thought. He only gave them water and a loaf of bread. But later I understood Abraham's obedience."

The Lord God promised to care for Ishmael, Tass explained, reading Genesis: "I will surely bless him; I will make him fruitful and will greatly increase his numbers. He will be the father of twelve rulers, and I will make him into a great nation" (Genesis 17:20; see also 21:13 NIV).

Tass confirmed my theory that the conflict that dominates the world is rooted in a story of rejection and two brothers who desperately wanted their father's love. Tass is committed to reaching the people who remain separated as a result of this ancient split. He reaches out to all—the Jews he once persecuted as well as Arab Christians and his former Muslim brothers.

Our first meeting was very emotional for me. We hugged and tears filled my eyes. It was like hugging Ishmael, a true son of Abraham. Tass had paid a huge price to follow God's call on his life, including alienation from his family. He gives me great hope. He knows that only God's love can bring peace to the Middle East. Tass has expanded my definition of "God's people."

Joel Rosenberg: "Am I Jewish?"

Botrus opened my eyes and gave me a deep appreciation for the Arab church. Tass reached into my heart and made the children of Ishmael real. But it took a Jew whose family hailed from the orthodox Brooklyn Jewish community to complete the picture and compel me to the "other side of the line," as he calls the Arab world. He's also a *New York Times* best-selling author and one of the smartest people I know.

I first met Joel Rosenberg through his books and became curious about this man who seemed to have prophetic inside knowledge about current events. His book *The Last Jihad* was written nine months before the terrorist attacks of

September 11, 2001. The book takes readers inside the cockpit of a hijacked plane being used on a suicide mission. I devoured the rest of his political thrillers as well as his 2006 book about prophecy and the Middle East: *Epicenter.* I felt compelled to meet this guy.

Joel intuitively understands the connection between current events and the Middle East. When I finally met him, I asked him to speak at our church. Another layer of knowledge and understanding about Israel began to unfold.

I asked Joel what it was like to grow up Jewish in America and then become a believer in Jesus.

"I didn't exactly grow up Jewish," he said. "My father very rarely talked about being Jewish. For him, growing up in an Orthodox Jewish home was not a positive. My grandfather was abusive, and my dad concedes that he was a terrible kid. It was a contentious and toxic situation."

Leaving Brooklyn and the Orthodox life behind, his father headed for his own promised land—La Jolla, California—where he studied to be an architect. Anything Gentile seemed good, and California was as far as he could get from Brooklyn.

Both his parents had come to faith in Christ, and since Joel's mother grew up as a Methodist, his family eventually joined a small Protestant church, where his dad started teaching an Old Testament Sunday school class. "But my father's Jewish background was never discussed," Joel recalls. "It was put away in a box, locked in a vault. My father's parents died before I was three, so I had no contact with my Jewish grandparents."

One day after church his dad announced he was planning a Passover Seder dinner for his fifth-grade Sunday school class, and he wanted the family to attend. "What's a Passover Seder?" Joel asked. After his father explained, Joel asked, "How would you know how to do that?"

"Well, because I'm Jewish."

Joel chuckled as he told me, "I was stunned! I practically shouted back at him, 'You're Jewish? Does this mean I'm Jewish? How did this never come up?'

"I must have been the dumbest kid in the class not to know I was Jewish. I mean, my name is Joel Rosenberg. But we never talked about it. It took me a while to get over the shock. And then I found out a lot of people grow up in America not knowing they are Jewish." He gave the example of Madeleine Albright, who didn't learn of her Jewish heritage until she was being vetted for secretary of state during the Clinton administration. Background checks revealed that many of her Jewish relatives in Czechoslovakia died in the Holocaust, including three grandparents.[4]

"A lot of people don't tell their kids, especially if they're immigrating," Joel explained. "They want to start with a clean slate—and they're afraid of anti-Semitism."

Over the years, Joel tried to pull information out of his dad, but with little success. "I had never heard of Jews for Jesus or Chosen People ministries. We didn't know any other Jewish believers. So I became curious: 'What do Jews believe about Jesus?'" During college, with his parents' support, Joel studied abroad at Tel Aviv University.

"Something opened up for me after being in Israel. I realized God has a plan and a purpose for this place. This is where Christ lived, where He is coming back. Israel is the vortex of everything biblical.

"I also realized," he said soberly, "that there's just not that many people on planet Earth right now who believe that Jesus is the Messiah. This became a big deal to me. I knew I was supposed to do something. I was supposed to seek a way to be a blessing to Israel and her people—and to share the good news of the Messiah."

·A Detour to the Other Side of the Line

Armed with new knowledge, a vision, and his own natural exuberance, Joel had a calling. He was even more certain when he met his wife.

"I met Lynn at Syracuse University. She was a creative-writing major and Jewish studies minor, and we were both students with Campus Crusade for Christ. It was perfect! She also loved Israel and the Jewish people, so when we got married, we knew that our lives would be involved in blessing Israel."

But God had a detour in store.

"He kept blocking our chances to go to Israel or minister. I was accepted to Hebrew University with a full scholarship, but our plans were thwarted by family events that made it impossible to leave. We were frustrated and confused. Then we started meeting Arab believers everywhere we went. We attended a missions conference at our church and met a couple who ran all the Campus Crusade ministries in the Arab world. Another couple managed an Arab-language radio ministry. We kept meeting Arab Christians, many overseeing huge ministries and deeply connected to the people of the Arab world. And we kept hearing about Muslims coming to Christ. More Muslims than Jews! The stories were incredible."

The years went by and still there were no open doors for the Rosenbergs to work in Israel—but totally open doors to minister to Arabs.

"In retrospect," Joel says, "it is very clear. The Lord was saying, *You are the Rosenberg family, and of course you are going to be a blessing and will minister in Israel. But I really want you to understand. I love Palestinians.... I need you to know and not just know in your head, but I want to sear into your heart and soul that I love the whole world, and that includes Israel's neighbors and enemies.*

"Neither Lynn nor I harbored any prejudice toward Arabs or antipathy toward Muslims. We were just ignorant. So for the first fifteen years of our marriage, we gained a new perspective."

By the summer of 2006, Joel knew it was time. He and Lynn launched The Joshua Fund, a nonprofit educational, humanitarian, and charitable organization reaching all the people of the Middle East. Every board member has either served on a mission trip to the Arab world or met Joel and Lynn while ministering in the Arab world. They all passionately love Israel, but they are equally committed to serving the Arab world.

Meanwhile, Lynn's sister married a Lebanese Christian who grew up in Beirut during Lebanon's civil war. "So it became personal," Joel said. "He's a brother in Christ. Personal relationships can certainly help shape one's view of how God loves people, especially people you might not normally know."

Justified Hurt

"We need to do a better job as the church and teach people that most Arabs and Muslims are not radical jihadists. We have brothers and sisters on the other side of the green line—and, yes, right in Israel. Which is why, when I write a novel, I include Arab, Iranian, and Muslim characters. Some are sympathetic, some heroic, some villains.

"When I was researching *Epicenter,* Lynn and I, our boys, and my mother-in-law lived in Egypt for three months. I wanted us to wake up every morning to the sound of Muslims being called to prayer. I wanted to see, feel, and understand the culture. Jesus doesn't simply tell us to love Muslims. He wants us to *go* love Muslims."

Each of these three men—Botrus, Tass, and Joel—have taught me to see the bigger picture. They have brought me deeper into the story of God's people. They have opened my heart to love the children of Isaac and Ishmael as God has always intended.

WHY ARE GOD'S CHOSEN PEOPLE SO HATED?

History's Most Persecuted People

I FIRST TRAVELED TO ISRAEL IN MAY 1982, JUST A month before violence erupted once again on the Lebanese-Israeli border. Incessant terrorist attacks and Israeli retaliation escalated to war.

For years I had desired to put my feet on Israel's land. Still captivated by prophecy, I studied current events and history. I wanted to see where it all started and where it all would take place in the near future.

I was now a married man with a family, and I was pastoring a church. At the age of twenty I had married Vicki, a beautiful young woman I had noticed at church in San Diego. Pastor Chuck ordained me, and I returned to my roots, El Cajon, where Vicki and I started a church, Calvary Chapel, El Cajon. Our church thrived, we were happy—but always there was the tug toward prophecy and Israel. When my chance finally came, no threat of terrorism or war would keep me from traveling to Israel.

The first time I walked along the Sea of Galilee, I felt connected to the land. I could picture Jesus teaching, surrounded by people. I saw Him healing the sick with a touch, inviting a child to sit with Him, telling His disciples where to cast their nets. As I looked out over the sea, there was Peter stepping out of his boat onto the water, walking toward Jesus. The familiar places and stories I had studied and taught materialized into real land, real people. These were the true flesh-and-blood brothers and sisters of Jesus the Messiah.

Tracing Today's Wars to an
Ancient Family Conflict

After additional visits to Israel, I began to understand the conflict that prevents peace and keeps this old-young nation on edge. On one visit a friend and I called a taxi to take us into Jerusalem. Our Arab driver described the sights and offered his own commentary.

When we got to the old city, he said, "This is where the cowboys live. You know, the black hats. Orthodox." He spit out the last word and gestured contemptuously out the window where black cloth flapped in the breeze as a group of orthodox Jewish men strolled past in their typical dress of dark short pants, white buttoned shirts, suit jackets, and black hats with wide brims.

This was relatively mild but still disturbing evidence of the hostility that divides this ancient city. The driver's disgust for Jews was tangible. In Israel, peace is hard to negotiate on a political level, but perhaps it's even more difficult in cities, neighborhoods, and disputed areas where Palestinians live.

It would be easy to see the geopolitical conflict only in light of historical battles over territory, ethnic strife fueled by long-held grudges, and the interference of foreign powers. But that is only part of the bigger story, which is that God chose the Jews and created a nation out of a people that, prior to His covenant, had not been a people. The ongoing hatred and war in the region is, above all, a spiritual struggle. And the issues involved are immense. The more immersed I became in Israel, the more I wanted to understand *why* the conflict between Jews and Arabs has persisted for centuries.

The modern Jewish-Arab conflict began with individuals whose names we know. It dates back to the Genesis account of God calling Abraham out of Ur and later the roles played by his sons and their descendants. Their personal struggles from thousands of years ago have become our struggles in the form of terrorism and war. The violence that kills antagonists and innocents alike can be traced back to sibling rivalry, marital strife, conflicts between generations, and political intrigue. The Bible records it all, and in studying the history and the prophecy found in Scripture it becomes evident that this is a spiritual battle, waged with righteous motives and deadly zeal.

Why Has the Church Opposed the Jews?

The Jews know the force of opposition that attempts to crush them as a people and as a nation. We aren't surprised when we read about the wars waged against Israel by ancient Gentile nations that originally occupied Canaan and the surrounding lands. In fact, we are inspired by the heroics of Joshua, David, and other warriors who led Israel into battle against seemingly superior armies.

But Israel has been attacked repeatedly for thousands of years with a relentless ferocity not endured by any other nation in history. And while in our time we tend to blame the Arab nations that insist Israel has no right to exist, the truth is that one of Israel's most adamant—and effective—opponents has been the church. Yes, Christians historically and today represent one of Israel's most consistent, most effective enemies.

I was invited to be part of a discussion at a Los Angeles synagogue along with radio talk-show host Dennis Prager and Rabbi Daniel Bouskila. We were to discuss the question "Are Christians Friends to the Jews?"

"For most of us the cross has been a sign of terror," the rabbi said. He was not overstating his case. The reality is, Christians are under suspicion. As I studied church history and the attitude of Christians toward Jews, I realized it is impossible to erase centuries of persecution and hatred from Jewish history or from the memories of today's Jews.

In the few minutes I had to speak at the synagogue, I attempted to explain that many Christians believe that our faith has its roots in the Jewish faith. I told them how grateful we are for this wonderful heritage and that we hold a special love in our hearts for Israel and her people. I told them that I am only beginning to comprehend the tragedies of the Holocaust and a host of other injustices done over centuries, often in the name of Christ. Some in the audience were Holocaust survivors. I asked for their forgiveness.

The response of Rabbi Bouskila's congregation was overwhelming. They applauded, they wept, then they rose to their feet in a standing ovation. I was unprepared for this. After the session, many from the congregation came up to talk and to express their appreciation. "I am stunned," a visiting rabbi kept saying. "We rarely clap during a service, and the only time we stand is to leave." I, too, was stunned and humbled to realize how much the thoughts I had expressed meant to these dear people.

This powerful encounter at a Sephardic synagogue is just one step in the relationship God is building between the Christian and Jewish communities. We still have a lot of evil and tainted history to overcome. The Jewish people are justified in their skepticism toward Christians. I wonder if the history of Christians' attitudes and actions against the Jews will shock you as much as it did me.

The Red Thread

Imagine the history of the human race as a giant tapestry, woven with millions of colored threads, creating thousands of complex patterns and scenes. The tapestry tells the stories of nations, families, and individual lives. Stand back as far as you can, and see how it all comes together to form a blended picture of life and humanity, with one exception.

Woven throughout is an extraordinary thread that stands out even in a color scheme as varied and complex as the human race. The thread disappears once in a while in the tangle of other threads, but it always turns up again, more bold, even defiant. It represents a tenacious little segment of humanity, a tiny bright thread that changes and upsets the bigger pattern and constantly rearranges the course of human events.

This thread is the Jewish people. I see them like a scene in the movie *Schindler's List*, shot in black and white, with one exception: a little girl in a red coat. In the bigness of the whole scene, you almost aren't sure what you are seeing, but you can't miss her. She changes not just one scene but the meaning of the story.

Through most of history the rest of the world didn't know what to do with this wild thread of humanity. Some ignore the Jews, dismissing them as an ancient people who should've disappeared. Some cultures have been driven to a demonic hatred of Jews, committing horrible atrocities in an attempt to exterminate them. But why has so much hatred and violence been directed at one tiny nation? And why has the church of Jesus Christ, of all people, often forsaken these brothers and sisters of Jesus?

I was shocked to discover how deeply the roots of anti-Semitism infiltrated the early church. Most are familiar to us—the Inquisition, Nazism, and other manifestations of prejudice and hatred directed toward the children of Israel. Many of the other anti-Semitic emphases and efforts, however, we have not heard of.

What Do We Do with the Gentiles?

The first-century church, a very Jewish group of people, wrestled with the question, What will we do with the Gentiles? You can see it in Acts 14–15. After reporting how God had opened the doors of faith to the Gentiles (that is, anyone who is a non-Jew), the debate began. The first Jewish believers agonized over whether to enforce circumcision, dietary laws, and other religious formalities on Gentile converts to Christianity. The church leaders ruled that non-Jews would *not* have to observe the entire Jewish Law. That decision, plus the missionary efforts of the apostle Paul to the Gentiles, caused the ethnic composition of the first-century church to change dramatically from a Jewish majority to a Gentile majority.

Gentiles began to change the face of the church, which did not defuse the tension. The politics of the day, especially after the destruction of the temple in AD 70, created an atmosphere of distrust and alienation between the early Christians and Jews who had not become believers in Yeshua. Eventually, Gentile believers began to look at their Jewish brothers and sisters with suspicion, and questions formed in their hearts and minds.

- Can the Jews really be saved just by grace, in defiance of their own laws? Do their laws and rituals need to be respected?
- Didn't the Jews reject Jesus?
- Did the Jews kill Jesus?

- Has God rejected the Jews? Can we trust them? Do we need to protect the world from them?

This has been a spiritual battle from the start. No wonder Paul wrote, "For our struggle is not against flesh and blood, but against the rulers, against the authorities, against the powers of this dark world and against the spiritual forces of evil in the heavenly realms" (Ephesians 6:12, NIV). Suspicion led to opposition, which led to teachings that singled out the Jews for targeted abuse. Then the question changed. The church began to ask, What will we do with the Jews?

A Dark, Evil History

How did the church, whose message is one of love and saving grace, become a hideout for hatred, prejudice, and persecution? How do people use God's Word to justify the Inquisition, slavery, prejudice, Nazism, anti-Semitism? When the church began to deny its Jewish heritage, prejudice slithered in. When that denial turned into persecution, the soul of the church darkened, and the door was opened to further atrocities.

The history is long and complicated, but here are a few highlights to give you an idea.

The Early Church
One of the earliest incidents of anti-Semitism in the church is found in 3 John. The apostle is concerned about Diotrephes's treatment of "the brethren." Diotrephes refused to welcome John and his fellow Jewish apostles and forbade anyone else to do so, threatening to put them out of the church (3 John 9–10).

The Separation of the Church and the Jews
Between AD 132 and 135 Simon Bar Kokhba, hailed by some Jews as the Messiah, led a successful revolt against the Roman Empire. He established an independent state of Israel that lasted more than two years, and then twelve Roman legions crushed the rebellion.

Thereafter, the Romans barred any Jews from Jerusalem, allowing them to return only to observe their day of mourning, Tisha B'Av. Jewish Christians did not support Bar Kokhba and did not believe he was the Messiah, but still they were barred from Jerusalem.

Dan Gruber wrote in *The Church and the Jews*:

> From the end of the Bar Kokhba rebellion on, all Jews were forbidden to even enter the precincts of Jerusalem.... Until that time, the bishops in Jerusalem had all been Jewish. If there were bishops in Caesarea before that time, they would have almost certainly been Jewish. The Roman Empire had destroyed or removed the Jewish bishops and churches. They were replaced by Gentile ones. The Gentile bishops and churches naturally began to think of themselves as having replaced the Jews.[1]

Justin Martyr

About AD 150 to 160, church father Justin Martyr, a Samaritan, expressed his belief that the destruction of Jerusalem and the suffering that followed was God's judgment for the Jews' failure to believe in Jesus.[2] From there an even larger step of flawed theology was taken, asserting that God had cast off the Jews and replaced them with the Gentile church. Justin wrote:

> And therefore all this has happened to you rightly and well. For ye slew the Just One and His prophets before Him, and now ye reject and, as far as in you lies, dishonour those that set their hope on Him, and God Almighty and Maker of the universe who sent Him, cursing in your synagogues them that believe on Christ.[3]

Justin believed that the church was the true Israel, but he did acknowledge the church's Jewish roots, believing that Gentiles had been grafted in. He wrote: "For even if you yourselves have ever met with some so-called Christians, who yet do not acknowledge this, but even dare to blaspheme the God of Abraham, and the God of Isaac, and the God of Jacob."[4]

Origen

Origen of Alexandria (AD 185–254) is known as the father of the allegorical method of biblical interpretation. He proposed replacing the literal interpretation of Scripture with allegories that, in his system, uncovered the *real* meaning of the text. "In this allegorical system," according to Dan Gruber, "when the text said, 'Israel,' it meant 'the Church' and not the Jews, so long as the promise or comment was good. If the promise or comment was not good, then 'Israel' still meant 'the Jews,' and not 'the Church.'"[5]

Eusebius

Then there was Eusebius in the fourth century. His *Ecclesiastical History of Eusebius Pamphilus* is the acknowledged history of the church from the end of the book of Acts to the Council of Nicaea. He had the writings of Justin and others who spoke of the millennium and kingdom to come, yet he did not want to make those writings known. Eusebius believed the church was the new Israel, replacing the Jews, and that God's plan included no distinct future for the Jews.[6]

His views were accepted into church thinking, and the churning tide swelled into anti-Semitism of tsunamic proportions.

The Passover Controversy

The trend toward separating Christianity and New Testament interpretation from its Jewishness finally colored the popular understanding of the gospel. The gospel centers on the death and resurrection of Christ, but controversy arose over which day should be set aside each year for a special celebration of the Lord's resurrection. Jesus celebrated Passover on the fourteenth day of Nisan because that is the date described in the Bible. He celebrated all the Levitical holy feasts on the days and in the manner that God decreed.

As we will discuss in a later chapter, the holy days are divine appointments. The apostles and the first-century church maintained these observances from Judaism, especially in light of the fact that the Lord's death and resurrection *coincided* with Passover! In the second century some churches in the West shifted the annual celebration of Passover-Easter so it always occurred on a Sunday. They ignored the biblical calendar and gave preference to the Roman calendar. The spring celebrations of the resurrection at Easter were stripped of the Passover's fixed date of the fourteenth of Nisan.

Daniel Gruber explains how this happened:

In some quarters the Church attempted to restrict the celebration [of Easter] to a single day, 14 Nisan; elsewhere—and this became the prevailing custom—she made Holy Week the week in which fell 14 Nisan (the day when the Jewish feast began), and removed the festival…to the Sunday following Holy Week…. Besides changing their dates, the Church also gave to the Jewish festivals, which she adopted, a purpose different from that which they had for the Jews. [Thus] Sunday commemorates the resurrection of the Lord, the victory over the Jews.[7]

Leaders in the early church kept pressing for their preferred shift in the date. Church authority from Rome brought the issue to the Council of Nicaea in AD 325.

Constantine's Sword

The Council of Nicaea, a gathering of prominent Christian leaders, often is heralded as the meeting that united Christendom under the watch of Emperor Constantine. What is not often acknowledged is that the council furthered the alienation of Christianity from its Jewish roots. The council ruled that all churches would celebrate the Passover, renamed Easter, on the ecclesiastically chosen Sunday rather than the date established in the Old Testament. Constantine sent a personal letter of exhortation to all the churches concerning this decision.

The emperor's words carried great weight. He ended the persecution of Christians and laid the foundation for the Holy Roman Empire. He professed the Christian faith as his own. He convened the council and endorsed its decisions with all the power of the state and its armies behind him.

What he wrote in his letter not only revealed his prejudices, especially against the Jewish people, but also changed the nature and course of the church for more than fifteen hundred years. In *The Ecclesiastical History of Eusebius Pamphilus*, we read:

> When the question arose concerning the most holy day of Easter, it was decreed by common consent to be expedient, that this festival should be celebrated on the same day by all, in every place. For what can be more beautiful, what more venerable and becoming, than that this festival, from which we receive the hope of immortality, should be suitably observed by all in one and the same order, and by a certain rule. And truly, in the first place, it seemed to everyone a most unworthy thing that we should follow the custom of the Jews in the celebration of this most holy solemnity, who, polluted wretches! having stained their hand with nefarious crime, are justly blinded in their minds.
>
> It is fit, therefore, that, rejecting the practice of this people, we should perpetuate to all future ages the celebration of this rite.... Let us then have nothing in common with the most hostile rabble of the Jews.... [L]et us withdraw ourselves, my much honored brethren, from that most odious fellowship...that the purity of your minds may not be affected by a conformity in anything with the customs of the vilest of mankind...these parricides and murderers of our Lord.... It is most religious and equitable that all should wish what the strictest reason seems to require, and to have no fellowship with the perjury of the Jews.[8]

Constantine did more than change the date for the celebration of the resurrection. He officially established an unscriptural, anti-Semitic foundation for the doctrine and practice of the church. He planted in the heart of the church the seeds of contempt for Jews and a clear separation from them as the only proper Christian attitude. This root of bitterness, planted just as the church and state merged in ancient Rome, would in the far future bear bitter fruit, including the Holocaust.

After the conclusion of the Council of Nicaea, Constantine held a banquet to establish and memorialize what had just taken place. Eusebius described the proceedings:

> No one of the bishops was absent from the imperial banquet.... The guards and soldiers, disposed in a circle, were stationed at the entrance of the palace with drawn swords. The men of God passed through the midst of them without fear, and went into the most private apartments of the royal edifice. Some of them were then admitted to the table of the emperor, and others took the places assigned to them on either side. It was a lively image of the kingdom of Christ, and appeared more like a dream than a reality.[9]

This raises an important question: Why didn't the leaders of the church, who had just completed a historic church council, raise objections to Constantine's hatred of the Jews? Did they consider raising their voices in defense of the Jews but then notice the "drawn swords"? Or were they willing to trade fidelity to the Scriptures for the entrapments of prestige?

A remnant did not go along with Constantine's council, and the stand they took led to a lasting separation. For a millennium, the sword of the state enforced the government's version of church doctrine. Later would come the Crusades, then the Inquisition, and even later, to those who dared to call for reform, there would be the blood of martyrs.

Bringing the church back to being the true bride of the Messiah would be a very long journey. And even some of the reformers who sought to overcome the most egregious abuses of the Roman Catholic Church were in error on their teachings regarding the Jews.

Martin Luther and the Holocaust

Fast-forward several centuries to Martin Luther, whom Sherwood Wirt called "the most important European of the past thousand years."[10] In spite of his numerous accomplishments and the stand he made for God's grace, to some Luther carries an unfortunate title: theologian of the Holocaust.[11]

Luther held some sympathy for the Jews in his early years. After he took a fiery stand against the Roman Catholic Church, he believed the Jews of his day would easily convert to Christianity. When they didn't, he grew bitter and launched a campaign against them. He made written accusations and false assertions that later were used by Nazi Germany to justify the Holocaust.

Luther's *Commentary on Romans* is considered one of the most influential books of Western civilization. It formed a major part of the foundation on which the Reformation is built. Yet in it and in other portions of Luther's works are some very disturbing comments. In his anger over the Jews' failure to convert, Luther wrote: "The Jews arrogantly assumed that they were God's people, simply because the heathen were not His people."[12]

Though Jesus, all the apostles, and all the early believers were Jewish, Luther had his own analysis: "They are real liars and bloodhounds who have not only perverted and falsified the entire Scriptures from beginning to end."[13]

In his *Commentary on Romans,* Luther's statement on 11:28 ("Concerning the gospel they are enemies for your sake") regarding the Jewish people is telling: "The word *enemies* must here be taken in a passive sense; that is, they deserve to be hated. God hates them and so they are hated by the Apostles and all who are of God."[14]

It is not my intent to be sensational but rather to urge all believers in Jesus to carefully examine their attitudes toward Jews. Tragically, Luther went even further. In an inflammatory tract published in 1543, he wrote:

First, their synagogues should be set on fire, and whatever does not burn up should be covered or spread over with dirt so that no one may ever be able to see a cinder or stone of it. And this ought to be done for the honor of God and of Christianity in order that God may see that we are Christians, and that we have not wittingly tolerated or approved of such public lying, cursing and blaspheming of his Son and his Christians.... Secondly, their homes should likewise be broken down and destroyed.... Thirdly, they should be deprived of their prayer books and Talmuds.... Fourthly, their rabbis must be forbidden under threat of death to teach any more.... Fifthly, passport and traveling privileges should be absolutely forbidden to Jews.... Sixthly, they ought to be stopped from usury.... Seventhly, let the young and strong Jews and Jewesses be given the flail, the axe, the hoe, the spade, the distaff, and spindle, and let them earn their bread by the sweat of their noses. To sum up, dear princes and nobles who have Jews in your domains, if this advice of mine does not suit you, then find a better one so that you may all be free of this insufferable devilish burden, the Jews.[15]

Adolf Hitler and the Nazi leadership took Luther's words and carried them out to the next horrifying level. Julius Streicher, a Nazi propagandist and editor of an anti-Semitic publication, argued during his trial in Nuremberg after World War II that if he should be standing there and arraigned on such charges, then so should Martin Luther.[16]

Hitler wrote in *Mein Kampf,* "I believe that I am acting in accordance with the will of the Almighty Creator: by defending myself against the Jew, I am fighting for the work of the Lord."[17] In 1938 Hitler repeated those words in a Reichstag speech.

The Root and the Branches

God chose the people who would be His, and He never wavered from that choice. In Romans 2:10, Paul wrote, "But glory, honor, and peace to everyone who works what is good, to the Jew first and also to the Greek." God honored the Jews first. As Jesus said to the woman of Samaria, "Salvation is of the Jews" (John 4:22).

The Jews represent humanity in general, with the same potential for faith and obedience and the same tendency to rebel and to be unfaithful to God. They are the prodigal son of history, falling into every human sin. They are a testimony of the battle between the flesh and the spirit. God, in His dealings with the Jews, has shown us His faithfulness in spite of our unfaithfulness.

Humanity's rejection of God's chosen people bore evil fruit through many centuries of hatred, prejudice, and persecution of the Jews. For the last two thousand years, the church has shown more judgment than mercy to them. Our fascination with them has been detached from genuine love, concern, and action taken to defend both the Jews and the nation of Israel. It is time to correct our sinful neglect—and even opposition—to the Jews. We can start righting the wrongs by following God's command: "Comfort, yes, comfort My people!" (Isaiah 40:1). The prophet was writing to the Hebrews, but today the Lord is speaking to the church: "Comfort My people, the Jews."

In his letter to the Roman church, Paul wrote, "For I do not desire, brethren, that you should be ignorant of this mystery, lest you should be wise in your own opinion, that blindness in part has happened to Israel until the fullness of the Gentiles has come in. And so all Israel will be saved" (Romans 11:25–26). The "blindness in part" has happened to the church as well. But now the Lord is opening the eyes of His bride, the church, to her Jewish roots.

If believers are willing to make a heartfelt investment in the people whom God has chosen to love unconditionally, He promises we will see a mighty work in the hearts of the Jewish people. I have seen examples of just that. My passion and prayer is that my brothers and sisters in the church will fall in love with the Jewish people. One day "all Israel" will know the love of Jesus through His body, the church, and embrace Him as their Messiah.

The fate of the world turns right now on the battle between those who passionately hate the Jews and those who fiercely love them.

Tracing Israel's Destiny Through the Ninth Day of Av

THE NINTH DAY OF AV ON THE JEWISH CALENDAR remains a mysterious date. On that date several years ago, August 15, 2005, trucks laden with furniture and supplies rumbled out of the Gaza Strip preparing to evacuate more than eighty-five hundred Jews. This was the deadline enforced by the Israeli government. It was just one more heart-wrenching event associated with this date.[1]

I was watching the news when images of Jews packing up, some being forcibly removed from their homes, filled the television screen. A stark contrast was presented by tens of thousands of cheering Palestinians. My heart was torn as I again confronted the agonizing issues both factions face.

"Do you see what's happening?" my friend Mark Biltz asked. "And it's Tisha B'Av." This date corresponds with a day of mourning. It is the holy day when observant Jews mourn and remember with deep sadness and solemn respect the drastic events that have shaped their national consciousness—and even their faith. Tisha B'Av commemorates two of the most tragic events in Jewish history: the first two times the temple was leveled—in 586 BC and AD 70. At least ten other major events have befallen the Jews on the ninth of Av. Some might regard this as eerie coincidences. The Jewish people do not.

The destruction of the first temple, built by Solomon, not only altered the course of Jewish history but also set the Jews on a path that would coincide again and again with world-changing events. Historically and in modern times, what befalls the Jewish people affects the rest of the world.

Writing about Tisha B'Av, Jewish columnist Sara Yoheved Rigler said:

We misrepresent the tragedy of the day by describing it as the destruction of the two Holy Temples, as if the catastrophe is the loss of a building. The American people do not mourn on 9/11 because of the destruction of the Twin Towers; they mourn the thousands of lives lost.... Tisha B'Av is more like a death than a destruction, because on that day the world changed irrevocably.[2]

Destruction of the Temples

A series of wicked kings led Israel away from God, leading to new levels of evil committed by the nation's leaders. The kings' rebellion set in motion a series of developments that weakened Israel, and eventually Jerusalem fell into the hands of Nebuchadnezzar, the Babylonian king. In spite of the prophet Jeremiah's warnings, in spite of numerous divine interventions, the people continued to reject God and despise His prophets. The Jewish leaders and priests took the lead in turning the people to idolatry. Finally God's judgment fell: "They mocked the messengers of God, despised His words, and scoffed at His prophets, until the wrath of the LORD arose against His people, till there was no remedy" (2 Chronicles 36:16).

Jerusalem fell victim to even more destruction and looting and widespread executions of the populace. A captain of the Babylonian army finally brought down the temple on the ninth of Av, 586 BC. Jerusalem's city walls were battered; the temple was stripped of all gold, silver, and precious metals. One hundred thousand Jews were slaughtered, and millions more exiled. The city was reduced to ashes.[3]

For seventy years Jewish exiles wept by the rivers of Babylon, captives in a strange land, crying, "If I forget you, O Jerusalem, let my right hand forget its skill!" (Psalm 137:5). Jeremiah earned his reputation as the weeping prophet because he witnessed this tragedy. His words reflect the personal and national sorrow felt at the terrifying judgment of God, which used the power of Babylon as His weapon of judgment.

Seventy years later Zechariah described Tisha B'Av as the fast of the fifth month (see Zechariah 7:3), a time of separation. Through weeping, mourning, and fasting, the people commemorated their tragic history. Six centuries later on the ninth of Av, AD 70, the stigma of this date was reinforced. Two million Jews died that day, and another million were exiled when a Roman army led by Titus destroyed the second temple. Today only a small section of that glorious temple remains, known as the Western Wall. Jews and Christians still go there to pray and weep for the tragedies that have befallen God's people.

A Series of Tragic Events

The expulsion of Jewish settlers from Gaza is the latest episode of displacement and heartbreak on Tisha B'Av. In contrast, the first such tragedy on this date took place on the ninth of Av, 1312 BC. On that date Moses sent twelve spies across the Jordan River and into Canaan to spy out the land.[4] Two of the spies, Joshua and Caleb, reported that the land was flowing with milk and honey. Standing before Moses and the people, Caleb exhorted, "We should go up and take possession of the land, for we can certainly do it" (Numbers 13:30, NIV). But the other ten spies saw only through eyes of fear: "The land...devours its inhabitants.... There we saw the giants...and we were like grasshoppers in our own sight, and so we were in their sight" (Numbers 13:32–33).

Fear spread through the encampment. The people's hearts turned away from the Lord. They wandered in the wilderness for forty years, missing the Promised Land because they did not believe. A pattern was established that has marked the ninth of Av to this day.

Here are some of the remarkable events that coincide with the ninth of Av:

- On August 4, AD 135, the Roman emperor Hadrian crushed the Bar Kokhba revolt. The city of Betar—the Jews' last stand against the Romans—was captured and liquidated. More than one hundred thousand Jews were slaughtered. The Roman general Tineius Rufus plowed under the temple area and its surroundings. Jerusalem was rebuilt as a pagan city and renamed Aelia Capitolina. Access was forbidden to Jews.

- The ninth of Ave fell on July 25, 1290, when all Jews were expelled from England for the "crime" of being Jewish.

- The Spanish Inquisition culminated with the expulsion of all Jews from Spain on Tisha B'Av in 1492. Hundreds of thousands of Spanish Jews were commanded to convert or be burned at the stake. The persecution uprooted and destroyed one of the largest Jewish communities of all time.

- World War I broke out on the eve of Tisha B'Av, August 1, 1914, when Germany declared war on Russia. German resentment from the war set the stage for the Holocaust, which began with Hitler's rise to power in the 1930s.

- On the eve of Tisha B'Av 1941, Reinhardt Heydrich was ordered to carry out the "final solution"—the extermination of all Jews in Europe.

- On the eve of Tisha B'Av 1942, the mass deportation of Jews from the Warsaw Ghetto to Treblinka began.

- August 14, 2005 (the ninth of Av), eighty-five hundred Jews were expelled from their homes in Gush Katif on the Gaza Strip.

The month and day that correspond with nine Av shift in the Gregorian calendar, which is based on the sun. But in the biblical calendar, based on both the sun and the moon, they remain constant. All these tragic events occurred on the same day through the ages.

Every nation has moments that change it forever—December 7 and September 11 are two watershed moments in American history. Jewish people are deeply aware of how historical events have changed and shaped their destiny. Their identity in the world has been formed and patterned by the events of Tisha B'Av.

As Christians choose to honor the roots of their faith, we stand with the Jewish people before the Father in heaven and pray for the prophet's words to be fulfilled:

> To console those who mourn in Zion,
> To give them beauty for ashes,
> The oil of joy for mourning,
> The garment of praise for the spirit of heaviness;
> That they may be called trees of righteousness,
> The planting of the LORD, that He may be glorified. (Isaiah 61:3)

Meeting the Israelis from Ezekiel's Prophecy

THE CHURCH I PASTOR IN SAN DIEGO DOES WHAT IT can to bless the Jewish people. In line with that, we sent Pastors Rick Hobson and Glenn Hirashiki to Sudan with a stop in Israel on their return. When they landed in Tel Aviv, a steady stream of violence had reduced Israeli tourism to nearly zero. "We got off the plane, obviously two Americans, and immediately we were surrounded by cab drivers looking for fares," Glenn said. "When we told them we needed a ride to Ariel, they scattered like we were radioactive. People were getting shot on the road to Ariel."

It was early 2001, and the Palestinian Intifada, initiated by Yasir Arafat and launched September 28, 2000, brought unprecedented violence to the area. (*Intifada* is defined as an uprising of Palestinian Arabs against the state of Israel. Before this four-year uprising formally ended, the death toll exceeded six thousand.[1])

Eventually a man approached them, saying his sister lived near Ariel so he could try to drive them. They prayed as their driver maneuvered to avoid the shooting areas, dodging in and out of olive groves and through jagged canyons. Between watching for snipers and hurtling over bone-rattling roads, Rick and Glenn both wondered if they would survive the trip. As they rolled up to a checkpoint, having no idea how or where this trip would end, the guards fired questions at them that they couldn't answer. All they knew for sure was they were supposed to meet Ron Nachman.

"Do you even know who he is?" the guards asked. They didn't know that Ron was the mayor of Ariel, a small Israeli city that had been established in the contested West Bank.

Their driver continued on, following vague directions to Ron's office. They hunted for a place that looked official and finally pulled up to a trailer in the wilderness of Samaria. Dina Shalit stepped out of the trailer and said, "You are here to see the honorable mayor of Ariel? Come in. Sit down. He'll be back soon."

"Ron arrived," Rick recalled, "with at least four cell phones on his belt. A busy, energetic, competent man who also turned out to be humble and gracious." Glenn and Rick had brought Ron a gift from our church. Touched by the gift and the fact they had traveled so far to meet him, Ron invited them to his home. His wife, Dorit, was out for the evening, so it was just the men. After a quick tour of his modest condo and the orchids he loves to grow, Ron barbecued some food for dinner.

Cuban cigars followed. "Now, tell me, why are you here?" Ron asked his guests. "Tell me about your church and your people on the west bank of America." Rick and Glenn tried to convey the strong support for Israel that characterizes many American Christians. Ron listened, thinking everything through, and ended the evening with an invitation for his visitors to see the city of Ariel the next morning.

Rick and Glenn stayed at the hundred-room Eshel Hashomron Hotel, where they were the only guests. This is the hotel with a crater in the front lobby. The hotel manager stopped a suicide bomber from doing even more damage. That night this local hero, managing the hotel by himself, also served as the bell clerk, cook, and night watchman. While Rick and Glenn tried to sleep, the hotel manager stood guard outside their room, armed to defend them against any attackers.

The next day Ron not only gave them a tour of his city but also arranged for lunch with former Israeli prime minister Benjamin Netanyahu. He met them at an elementary school, where they took pictures with some of the students. On their return trip to Tel Aviv, Rick and Glenn wore bulletproof vests. There was only one shooting incident en route, when snipers hit the car traveling behind them. "They checked our vehicle for bullet holes afterward and decided everything was okay, so we went to lunch," Rick said. By that time he was too exhausted to worry.

It turned out that Ron Nachman later had business in the United States, so he included a side trip to California for a meeting with me and some of my staff. Based on my reading about Israeli settlements in the West Bank—plus Rick and Glenn's report from Ariel—I knew that Ron was a leader who was passionately and tirelessly devoted to his people. My first meeting with him changed my life.

Joining in the Fulfillment of Prophecy

Ron was six years old in May 1948 when the Jews returned to their homeland. But the memories begin even earlier. "When I was three years old," he said, "I remember my family watching the British trains coming into Israel with prisoners of war who had been released by the American armies and allies in Europe. Among them were my relatives who had fought in Europe against the Nazis." His family would sit by the rails, sometimes until nightfall, waiting for a train to round a curve in the tracks. "Sometimes we would wait, and no one we knew would get off. We were disappointed.... We waited some more, and perhaps on the next train we would meet our relatives."

Then came November 29, 1947. Resolution 181, the official UN act to partition Palestine, as recommended by the majority of the United Nations Special Committee on Palestine (UNSCOP), allotted the new Jewish state a small part of western Palestine and recognized the right of the Jewish people to a state, not just a "national home" as stated in the 1917 Balfour Declaration and the 1922 Mandate for Palestine.[2]

Ron remembers the announcement. "I was five years old, but I remember the night [in 1947]. We listened to the news [on a radio], and though I didn't exactly understand the United Nations or Resolution 181, I knew something wonderful had happened for my people, my family." On May 14, 1948, the British mandate over Palestine expired. A proclamation was approved, declaring the establishment of the state of Israel. The United States recognized the new nation that same night.

"I remember it all," Ron continued. "The celebration, the joy, the happiness, the dancing in the street. Then, immediately, the very next day the riots began. Arabs against Jewish people. In my hometown there was only one road to exit and enter, like the Wild West. An Arabic school sat at the only entrance, and people started shooting along the road. My people were armed because we had no army, because we had no state until then. Each family had at least one person carrying a pistol. We called them civil guards, and their job was to protect Jewish people as they traveled on this road. They [the Arabs] tried to push us out even then. So peace never came. Peace never came."

The young boy who had witnessed so much joy and celebration over the rebirth of the nation of Israel, followed by the terror of continuing conflict, grew up with the state of Israel. His identity was completely wrapped up in the betterment and growth of Israel. His heritage was Zionism.[3]

"You see, I come from a very famous Jewish family," Ron said, "like the *Mayflower* families in America. My grandfather (Jeremiah Boxer) was the head of his city, Nes Ziona, for thirty-five years. My father (Ze'ev Nachman) was deputy mayor for fifteen years. I grew up in this ambitious family, but I had no idea what I would do. I am a fourth-generation *sabra*."

Sabra, the term used to describe Jews born in Israeli territory, comes from the name of a thorny, tenacious desert plant, a prickly pear. These plants grow in an arid climate and are tough on the outside, soft and sweet on the inside. *Yes,* I thought, *Ron's a sabra.*

Ron married Dorit. He earned a degree in political science and then a law degree from Tel Aviv University. He and Dorit began raising a family, which grew to four daughters. By 1970 he was working for the Israeli Defense Industries. He recalls in 1972, when the minister of defense, Moshe Dayan, approached the young generation of Israel. "He appealed to us, saying we needed to hold two flags. The flag of defense and security and the flag to renew the spirit of Zionism, which meant to try to settle in [the disputed] areas like the Sinai, Gaza, and the Golan Heights."

Already working for the defense department, Ron met Dayan's second challenge by thinking of ways to build his country. He started with what became known as the Tel Aviv nucleus, people who would eventually become the first citizens of Ariel.

"Every day I went to work for Israel defense until 4 p.m. Then I would go to the university until 6 p.m. to study law, and every night I would go to a parlor meeting, schlepping all over the country to convince people to join the nucleus."

Dorit was pregnant while he was keeping up this frenetic schedule. "I had to take myself to the hospital when the time came [to deliver their first child]," she said. "He met me there, but when the doctor said three more hours, he said, 'I'll be back.'" Their first child was born twenty-five minutes later. Dorit laughed. "He was so surprised!"

Building a Nation

The Nachmans worked together to build their homeland. Sometimes the nucleus meetings were held in their tiny apartment in Tel Aviv, and soon there were two baby girls.

"The adventure began in 1972," Ron said, "but was interrupted by the Yom Kippur War [in 1973]. [Henry] Kissinger was secretary of state, remember? Our efforts [to establish settlements in Samaria] stopped because the priority of Israel was to exist, to survive. It was a very up-and-down time, and thousands died on all sides."

Ron explained that by 1977 the Israeli government, in agreement with the United States, determined that Israel needed six outposts for security—and one of them was to be situated on a lot in Samaria. In political circles and in debates at the United Nations, disputed territory is said to be "occupied" by Israelis. Israeli settlements are said to be illegal; Israeli citizens are said to be squatters or worse. Such settlements are said to violate the Palestinians' territorial rights.

"We are not outlaws!" Ron emphasized. "We are not occupiers. The land was given to us with permits and was not owned by private parties. No one was here. First, the government approved the nucleus, then we were given a legal permit that recognized us as having the right to settle on this land. Everything is written in documents. We wanted no conflict with [the] government of Israel. We are not zealots who go running from mountain to mountain planting outposts. We did not take the land from anyone. It was undeveloped property."

The Sound of Rattling Bones

Ron is a leader of his people, working not only to establish the reborn homeland of the Jews, but also to carry out what God had promised thousands of years earlier through the prophets. Ezekiel, in his visions, saw Ron Nachman and others doing the work that is taking place today.

Dry bones, the Old Testament prophet said. Ezekiel prophesied that dry bones would rattle loudly and come "together, bone to bone" (Ezekiel 37:7). The prophet continued: "Indeed, as I looked, the sinews and the flesh came upon them, and the skin covered them over; but there was no breath in them" (verse 8).

Ron knows these prophecies better than almost anyone, in part because he shouldered the responsibility to take the risks and do the work to see that God's promise was fulfilled. The prophet added, "These bones are the whole house of Israel" (verse 11).

Ezekiel's prophecy has been unfolding for decades. As a young boy, Ron saw the "rattling" of a horrific world war to stop an evil dictator who set out to rid the earth of Jews. Six million Jews were killed before the Allies ended the Third Reich. Out of that evil a mighty rattling of bones reconnecting and rising was heard around the world. Jews came from the corners of the earth to put sinews and flesh and skin on the skeleton of this ancient, dispersed, and fragmented nation. But the prophet said, "There was no breath in them" (verse 8).

Now, Ron Nachman and others are establishing outposts in Israel. He is determined to breathe life into his nation and his people.

The Pioneers Described in Prophecy

"Prophesy to the breath, prophesy, son of man, and say to the breath,…'Come from the four winds, O breath, and breathe on these slain, that they may live.'… [A]nd they lived, and stood upon their feet, an exceedingly great army" (verses 9–10).

In the months before Ron and a squad of Israeli soldiers set up some tents in the hills of Samaria, he was planning, organizing, and writing out his vision for a city. "We started with nothing," he recalled. "We established everything from scratch."

There would be no roads and little infrastructure. They pitched two tents on a hill, and over the next year Ron honed his vision, wrote it out in detail, and sent it to the prime minister. Each paragraph described a different aspect of his plan, from how to pick the people who would settle there to deciding the size of the town, outlining plans for building industry and providing education and community services.

"We needed teachers, nurses, drivers, all kinds of professions and skills and the ability to integrate all of them," Ron explained. "We needed strong people. We didn't care if they were rich or poor, but they needed to be mentally healthy, willing to be part of a community. People willing to work with others and psychologically able to live without modern comforts for a period of time." Dorit added, "People with patience."

Ron opened the door to immigrants, especially Russian immigrants who were pouring into Israel. They were, as the prophet foretold, "coming from the four winds" (verse 9).

The community grew, but at first the settlers were men and unmarried workers. Family members would visit once a week to see what was being accomplished. "Every Saturday," Dorit said, "was like a pilgrimage. There was no road yet, so we took a convoy of trucks, Jeeps, whatever could handle the terrain, through the wilderness. Every family brought food to share, and we [the settlers] got to know each other's wives and children."

On one day when the visitors had come, Ron led them on a tour of the future Ariel. "He was jumping from rock to rock," Dorit said, "and every few feet he would stop and wait for us to catch up, then exclaim, 'You see this rock? Here will be a school. See this rock? A clinic!' " With his followers gasping as they tried to keep up, he showed them his vision and energized their community. He was not describing a dream but a certain reality.

"Everything happened just the way he said it would," Dorit concluded.

Soon the Saturday-only visits were over. On a Sunday in August 1978 a convoy of fifty-six trucks brought fifty-six families to Ariel. They lived in trailers for three years, often lacking electricity when the generators were spent, struggling to import food and precious water, which was supplied by tanker trucks. Ariel's right to exist was under international scrutiny. Violence was a constant threat.

But even so, Dorit recalls those early days as "wonderful." When their permanent home was built, she went upstairs and looked out over the city. "I saw this growing community where there had only been rocks and olive trees. It was like opening the Bible and reading about the early Israelites." She is a woman of incredible strength and generosity, willing to do her part in fulfilling Ron's vision, which echoes that of the ancient prophet Ezekiel:

"Behold, O My people, I will open your graves and cause you to come up from your graves, and bring you into the land of Israel.... I will put My Spirit in you, and you shall live, and I will place you in your own land. Then you shall know that I, the LORD, have spoken it and performed it," says the LORD. (verses 12, 14)

Ron thought a moment about the pioneers he had led to found the city. He asked with a shrug, "Why? How did we do it? Perhaps it is the Almighty, guiding me without me knowing. Yes, perhaps it is the Almighty."

Israel's Once and Future Leader

AS EZEKIEL'S PROPHECIES WERE BEING FULFILLED by pioneers such as Ron and Dorit Nachman, God was speaking to an African Christian, Robert Mawire, about the leadership of modern Israel. Mawire is the man who had arranged my initial meeting with Ron, and he is the brave man who had a second word to deliver to a leader of Israel.

Benjamin Netanyahu was scheduled to visit the United States in 2001, and Ron Nachman realized the former prime minister could do much to cultivate solidarity with Israel among American Christians. So he asked two American pastors, my associates Rick and Glenn, if they could set up a meeting at which Netanyahu could speak to a large audience of American Christians.

Rick and Glenn called me from Ariel with the idea, and we set in motion the process of scheduling an event at Calvary Chapel in Fort Lauderdale, Florida. The location tied in with Netanyahu's travel itinerary, and South Florida has a large Jewish population. Now all I had to do was call the pastor, Bob Coy, to see if he would help us pull this off in just two weeks. It took me five minutes to convince him I wasn't kidding.

The event was set for April 16, and Bob's staff went into overdrive, coordinating with the US State Department and Israel's security team. What Netanyahu didn't know was that, in addition to speaking to a capacity audience in South Florida, he would be receiving a second prophecy from Robert Mawire.

We arrived at the church where Netanyahu would be speaking. Security measures were in place, and tensions were high. Helicopters hovered overhead. Discreet, armed Mossad personnel (Israel's security force) infiltrated the crowds. Journalists and news helicopters joined the chaos. A large portion of the local Jewish community arrived to hear "Bibi," a hero to most of them. The church filled early, and guards kept the crowds orderly and away from the aisles and exits. Wide tape outlined an off-limits area in front of the stage. Anyone entering that zone was immediately confronted by security personnel.

We were ushered to the back of the church, to the green room where we met with Robert Mawire, Benjamin and Sarah Netanyahu, Rick, Glenn, Ron Nachman, Bruce Johnston, Dina, Bob Coy, and other members of his staff. Guards stood outside the door. We greeted one another and prayed together.

Netanyahu projects a strong presence. Born in Tel Aviv, he grew up in Jerusalem until his high school years, when his family moved to the United States. After high school he returned to Israel to join the Israel Defense Forces, where he proved his leadership and heroism. He returned to the United States and earned degrees from the Massachusetts Institute of Technology. He also studied political science at Harvard.

That day in 2001, while he was easy to talk to, he also seemed very deliberate and serious. I knew that the Lord had given Robert another message for the former and future prime minister, so I braced myself. Was this really the right time? How would Netanyahu receive the prophecy? He and Robert were friends now, but still, the boldness of it...

Robert stepped forward in the green room. He handed Netanyahu a plaque and read aloud the words inscribed on it:

The God of Abraham, Isaac, and Jacob has chosen you to be the "Father" of His people and to restore the Tabernacle of David. You will once again become Prime Minister of Israel, and God has appointed Ron Nachman to be your right hand man, as it was with Joshua and Moses.

If you honor His covenant that He made with Abraham, Isaac, and Jacob regarding Israel, He will honor you and exalt you. But if you disregard His covenant and give away His land, He will dishonor you.

"Be strong and of good courage: for unto this people shalt thou divide for an inheritance the land, which I sware unto their fathers to give them. Only be thou strong and very courageous, that thou mayest observe to do according to all the law, which Moses my servant commanded thee: turn not from it to the right hand or to the left, that thou mayest prosper whithersoever thou goest. Have not I commanded thee? Be strong and of good courage; be not afraid, neither be thou dismayed: for the LORD thy God is with thee whithersoever thou goest" (Joshua 1:6–7, 9 [KJV]).

—From the Servant of God, Robert Mawire, Fort Worth, Texas, 2001

We were quiet as Robert confirmed the message of the plaque, saying, "God is not done with you. You will be prime minister again at a critical time in history. Don't ever negotiate land for peace again."

Unlike his response to Robert's first prophecy in 1998, Netanyahu nodded seriously, accepting the words. He looked into Robert's eyes and thanked him. Then the program for the evening began with Bob Coy asking, "How do I introduce Moses?"

Enthusiastic applause greeted Netanyahu, and he acknowledged the many friends of Israel present, including the American pastors, his "good friend Ron Nachman, mayor of Ariel in the heart of Israel," and the Jews and non-Jews alike who are ardent supporters of Israel. "I think you know that there is a battle waging as we speak," he said, "and in this battle in which Israel fends off violence and terror, Israel will win. That's the first thing I can tell you."

Well into his speech he told the story of his visit to China a few years earlier. He had met with President Chen Shui-bian. They discussed the endurance of their two cultures, with the Chinese and the Jews representing two of the oldest civilizations on earth, dating back four to five thousand years. They added India to the category. Then Netanyahu asked the president, "How many Chinese are there in the world today?"

"One billion two hundred million."

"How many Indians?"

"About one billion one hundred million."

"Do you know how many Jews there are? Twelve million."

Netanyahu said, "You could hear a lot of Chinese jaws dropping in that room. After all, for them that's a tiny suburb of Beijing."

We laughed along with the audience, but he pressed his point: "What happened? A lot of things. But they boil down to one main thing. The Chinese kept China. The people of India kept India. But we Jews lost our land and were flung to the far corners of the earth, and from this dispersion came all our calamities and all the exiles and pogroms and massacres leading down to the greatest massacre of our time, the Nazi Holocaust.

"For two thousand years we have been trying to do one thing: rebuild our lives as a free, proud, independent people capable of defending ourselves."

It all comes down to the land and the miracle that Israel even exists. The Jewish homeland is not simply a symbol; it is a living nation and the fulfillment of prophecy. Netanyahu gave us a short history lesson based on the writings of Giovanni Battista Vico, an Italian historian who lived more than four hundred years ago. Vico tried to define the ironclad laws of history, one of which is this: all civilizations follow clear, predetermined, inexorable rules. Civilizations are born, they flower, they shrivel, then they die. If you wait long enough, Vico wrote, this happens to all civilizations. The evidence is recorded in every history book. Just look at the Sumerians, the Assyrians, the Byzantines, the Persians, the Greeks, and the Romans.

"Except," Netanyahu said, "for one exception. The Jews. The Jews refuse to die. And they have had the power and the faith to say every year, 'next year in Jerusalem, next year in Jerusalem,' and to never bend to these so-called iron laws of history. Because the Jewish people did something no other people has ever done.

"Many peoples have been displaced. All displaced people suffer one of two fates. They either fight wars and conquer new lands where they build new lives, or they are assimilated among the peoples with which they reside. But the Jewish people as a collective body refused to do either one. They refused to conquer new land for themselves, and they refused to be assimilated. Instead, they wanted to do something absolutely extraordinary. They wanted to go back. Back to the land, to the place that had forged their identity, that had forged their faith, where they found their inspiration for life. The land where the Bible was written.

"And to achieve this, we required deep reservoirs of faith that defy all rational analysis. And we did come back, to a barren land that we brought to life. Coming back meant returning to the ancient land of Judea and Samaria. In these hills you can close your eyes and picture our ancestors and our ancient prophets."

Getting ready to close his speech, Netanyahu said, "We will not knuckle under [to] others' aggression, we will not be suckered into giving up our lives and our land and our independence. We will never give up Jerusalem. This is where King David walked, where the kings of Israel walked, where the great prophets walked. This is where the Maccabees fought. This is the site of the holy Temple Mount. Jerusalem is mentioned in the Bible seven hundred times. This is our land, our city; it is ours by rights."

Finally, as the audience gave him a standing ovation, he said, "My friends, it is all of you standing up for Jerusalem and Israel that gives me confidence to follow the guidance of God to Joshua when he told him, 'Be strong and of good courage. Wherever you go I will go with you. We shall be strong and of good courage.'"[1] (He was paraphrasing Joshua 1:6, 9 and quoting the scripture Robert had read to him earlier in the green room.)

The former and future chief executive of Israel had reaffirmed an ancient prophecy. We had heard from another leader whom Ezekiel had seen in his vision of Israel's rebirth.

PART 4

GOD GIVES US SIGNS

Patterns and Predictions in Prophecy

FULFILLMENT OF PROPHECY IS NOT A STATIC FACT, like freeze-framing a scene in a movie. When we study the Hebrew prophets and plot their predictions on a time line, it's easy to focus only on the dramatic events. It is popular to speculate on the identity of the Antichrist, to spin out theories on what the mark of the Beast is and how it will be affixed on those who fail to claim the blood of the Lamb.

Amid all the study of Armageddon, the battle of Gog and Magog, the massive armies from the east, and blood reaching the bridles of horses on the field of battle, there is the living, ongoing fulfillment of prophecy. The Scriptures give us a macro-level look at how God will fulfill His plans. But it's a mistake to miss the truth of what is happening right now, every day in the Middle East. Prophecy is being fulfilled in a continual movement of people, circumstances, and decisions. These are the important details that occur between the major events described by the prophets. And these details, the ongoing movement toward the return of Jesus, are what I want Christians to understand and to be involved in.

Robert Mawire does more than simply study the ancient prophecies. He receives a word from the Lord and then takes the message to leaders who are positioned to act on God's message. Robert has shared a guiding principle that is useful in interpreting prophecy: "Look for those times when God repeats Himself. He is doing something very significant. He is trying to send us a message. He establishes patterns."

Robert's interpretive principle is echoed by Mark Biltz, a believer who teaches Scripture from the perspective of its Hebrew roots. "God speaks through patterns," Mark also told me. "Recognizing patterns in Scripture and history is to think with a Hebrew mind-set." Teachers, speakers, and writers do the same thing today. A classic structure for getting a point across is to tell your audience what you plan to say, say it, then review for your audience what you just told them.

Long ago I read J. Vernon McGee's comment that "prophecy is the mold into which history is poured."[1] What if the mold is not a simple, one-dimensional, linear time line? What if the testimony of the ancient prophets is not meant to be a checklist? What if our role is to do a lot more than try to identify predicted events and check them off as they occur?

McGee's comment regarding the "mold into which history is poured" might well be a multifaceted, multilayered picture of what God has done, is doing, and will do in the very near future. History, after all, sometimes repeats itself. But at the same time, history continues to surprise us. Leaders appear on the scene, and events unfold that are out of character and not what we expect. Unless we pay attention to the complexities of events, we will see only the surface of all that is happening to bring God's plans to fulfillment.

The Return of the Messiah

Why have so many respected Bible teachers fallen into a trap of predicting dates for the Lord's return only to be shown later to have been in error? This has happened repeatedly in the past century, and it never serves the cause of Christ or the reputation of His church. One reason it is so tempting to set dates is that we lean toward a linear reading of Scripture. We simplify prophecy to fit a certain system or to match a timetable or an expected sequence of events that makes sense to us. But what would happen if we set aside the focus on naming names and setting dates and instead sought to gain a deeper understanding of the patterns God has already revealed to us?

I discovered how patterns help explain history when I was reading a pictorial history of the Roman Colosseum. The ancient arena stands in ruins, of course, but the book described its magnificence and glory in ancient times. On one page an overlaying transparency allowed me to see the Colosseum in its glory. The arena came alive with brilliant color restoring its ancient beauty.

I realized that we often read the Bible as ancient history, drained of all life and color. Many concentrate on the ruins of antiquity as if the writings are locked into a past epoch that is interesting but not connected to our life and faith. We marvel at how God moved among the ancient Near Eastern tribes, but we fail to read the accounts of God's work through the overlay of God's patterns. We miss what these patterns reveal about God's character and plans for our lives and our world.

The difference between reading the Bible with a linear, Western mind-set and how the first-century Jewish teachers and leaders read—including Jesus and Paul—radically affects how we view prophecy. The Western mind sees prophecy as a written record of predictions and descriptions of how the predictions will unfold. Rather than backing up a few steps so we can see the bigger picture, we focus on separate events and try to line them up. The result is that we reduce prophecy to an event being foretold rather than seeking to understand the bigger pattern of what God is doing.

The Jewish mind understood prophecy differently. They were not bound by a Western tradition of seeking to impose order and structure on the narrative of Scripture. Instead, they saw prophecy as repeating patterns, with each event adding a new layer to the overall picture. As they studied God's patterns, they discovered richer and more profound meanings in the words of the prophets.[2]

Two concepts revolutionized how I read the Bible and can be especially helpful in reorienting our study of prophecy: learning to identify and read God's patterns, and applying the principle of "first natural, then spiritual."

Establishing Patterns

Paul, having been taught by the highly respected Rabbi Gamaliel (see Acts 22:3), wrote to the Christians in Corinth, "Now all these things happened to them [the Jews] as examples" (1 Corinthians 10:11). The Greek word for *example* means "impression, example, images, model, pattern."[3] God established patterns of events that we can study to understand the past *and* the future. Many prophecies have dual and sometimes multiple fulfillments. Prophecies of the past are also prophecies for the future. My pastor, Chuck Smith, said, "Prophecy is best understood after it has come to pass."

Sometimes a prophesied event is not recognized until after it has taken place. Hosea, speaking for the Lord, wrote, "When Israel was a child, I loved him, and out of Egypt I called My son" (Hosea 11:1). God called Israel out of Egypt during the Exodus. But we also know now that He was referring to His Son, the Messiah, about whom Matthew wrote some eight centuries later, "He took the young Child and His mother by night and departed for Egypt,...that it might be fulfilled which was spoken by the Lord through the prophet, saying, 'Out of Egypt I called My Son'" (Matthew 2:14–15).

The Lord established an intentional pattern. Predicting in advance how this prophecy would be fulfilled was impossible, but first-century Jews—such as Matthew—didn't look only at the facts of a prediction. They were also able to recognize a pattern revealed to them by the Holy Spirit.

God prophesied to Abraham that his descendants would be strangers in a foreign land, enslaved and abused for four hundred years (see Genesis 15:13). Hundreds of years later, a Pharaoh, determined to annihilate the promise of future generations of Hebrews, ordered the slaughter of all male babies born to Jewish mothers. Moses, the chosen deliverer, escaped because his mother hid him.

Matthew echoed the prophet Jeremiah: "Lamentation and bitter weeping, Rachel weeping for her children, refusing to be comforted for her children, because they are no more" (Jeremiah 31:15). In his gospel, Matthew recalls the same haunting lament in his description of Herod's vengeful murder of Bethlehem's male infants in the first century: "Lamentation, weeping, and great mourning, Rachel weeping for her children, refusing to be comforted, because they are no more" (Matthew 2:18). Jesus escaped the slaughter when Mary and Joseph fled with Him to Egypt.

In Israel's history, the pattern of deliverance is repeated: Esther and Haman, Daniel and Nebuchadnezzar. But the slaughter of innocents and the emergence of a deliverer from humble means form a picture whose layers grow deeper and richer as time moves closer and closer to the return of the Messiah.

Another Prophetic Pattern

I look at the rebirth of Israel in 1948 and recognize not only a fulfillment of prophecy but another layer of an established pattern. Israel has a long history of scattering and regathering, but with each cycle a vivid "transparency," like the overlay in my book about ancient Rome, is laid over the dim images of the ancient past. It gives us an increasingly clear picture of the coming of the Messiah. The fulfillment of prophecy is revealed in stages, not just by plotting points on a timetable.

Isaiah, writing in the eighth century BC, warned his people of impending captivity and the devastation of Israel. The destruction of Solomon's temple in 586 BC and the Babylonian exile fulfilled his prophecy. But Isaiah also predicted, "The LORD shall set His hand again *the second time* to recover the remnant of His people who are left, from Assyria and Egypt, from Pathros and Cush, from Elam and Shinar, from Hamath and the islands of the sea" (Isaiah 11:11). In other words, Isaiah says that God will gather His people from the four corners of the earth.

Allowed to return to their home by Cyrus the Great in 538 BC, the Israelites rebuilt their temple and reestablished their nation, creating the setting in which the Messiah would be born. With that cycle completed, Israel was again surrounded by enemies. In AD 70 the Romans destroyed Jerusalem, and the Jews were again dispersed, exiled from the land God had given them.

The Diaspora lasted almost two thousand years, until 1948 when the nation of Israel was reborn. Since that time, Israel has been surrounded by enemies committed to its destruction. And just as the pattern has revealed in the past, the stage is set again for the coming of the Messiah.

First Natural, Then Spiritual

The second guiding principle in reading prophecy through the lens of patterns is this: look first for the natural meaning of the Scripture and then for a spiritual meaning. This is something else I learned from Robert Mawire. "All prophecies must have a spiritual and material fulfillment in history," he said to me one day, stretching out his hands as if to take in all the physical manifestation around us. "What God does in the natural, He follows with the spiritual! Isn't it marvelous?"[4]

In 1 Corinthians 15:46, Paul explains one of the most consistent divine patterns in Scripture: "The spiritual is not first, but the natural, and afterward the spiritual." Once again, this approach runs counter to the Western mind-set. Aren't we supposed to be spiritual first and later see the fruit of that in the natural world?

Paul was speaking of the resurrection, but he also was teaching a new way of seeing and understanding. God has embedded spiritual truths in the natural world, and we will recognize those truths if we have "eyes to see." It makes sense that the sequence would be first natural and then spiritual. For example, because we have natural bodies, which we can see and feel, we can imagine having a spiritual body.

God called Israel the "apple of His eye" (Zechariah 2:8). In some mysterious way, when we look at Israel, we are looking into the eyes of God. When we look at Israel, we see God's intentions for the world. The dry bones came together as Ezekiel prophesied. The "sinews and the flesh" covered the bones and gave them physical substance. The nation was reborn, restored to its natural state. But there was "no breath," Ezekiel observed (see Ezekiel 37:8).

God is now breathing life into the Jews and others who have returned to the Holy Land. The number of Israeli believers in Yeshua the Messiah is growing daily. Yeshua has entered into the beliefs and consciousness of both devout and secular Jews and Arabs. Sometimes it occurs suddenly, for example, in a dream, a vision, or a revelation. Other times Yeshua becomes real in a fresh look at the Scriptures and a realization of the prophecies that He fulfilled.

Joel Rosenberg has cited statistics that there are approximately 15,000 Messianic Jews in Israel and 350,000 in the United States.[5] Tom Doyle, longtime missionary in the Middle East, wrote a remarkable book titled *Dreams and Visions,* chronicling the stories of hundreds of Muslims who have embraced Jesus as their Savior and Messiah.

Israeli believers who love Yeshua serve in the IDF, teach in schools, manage businesses, and serve in politics, law, and numerous ministries. Some are Jewish, others Arab. They infuse life into their land with their faith. And those who do not yet recognize Jesus as the Messiah are forming strong friendships and alliances with Christians. These are active citizens, entrepreneurs, leaders. They are involved in the physical rebuilding of Israel, and now many are engaged in the spiritual renewal of the people of Israel. First the natural and then the spiritual.

When you join in with the work of rebuilding Israel, even on a limited basis, you cannot escape the commitment and courage of the Israelis who are putting everything on the line. They take great risks to establish a secure, flourishing, free homeland. I have mentioned my interactions with Benjamin Netanyahu and Ron Nachman. Allow me to insert here a vignette of these men, not in a political or public setting, but as men whose hearts are devoted to their people and their country.

Cancer and Auschwitz

The year my friend Ron Nachman was diagnosed with cancer, the world changed in immeasurable ways. The United States inaugurated Barack Obama as our forty-fourth president in 2009. Two months later Benjamin Netanyahu was sworn in on March 31, for the second time, as prime minister of Israel. He returned to office after a ten-year gap, just as Robert Mawire had predicted.

Several months later, in January 2010, Netanyahu journeyed to Poland to commemorate the sixty-fifth anniversary of the liberation of the Nazi death camp at Auschwitz. In a speech that expressed grief, anger, and a determination to "never forget," the prime minister reminded the world of the prophecy of Ezekiel 37:

> The Jewish people rose from ashes and destruction, from a terrible pain that
> can never be healed. Armed with the Jewish spirit, the justice of man, and the

vision of the prophets, we sprouted new branches and grew deep roots. Dry bones became covered with flesh, a spirit filled them, and they lived and stood on their own feet.

As Ezekiel prophesized:

"Then He said unto me: These bones are the whole House of Israel. They say, 'Our bones are dried up, our hope is gone; we are doomed.' Prophecy, therefore, and say to them: Thus said the Lord GOD: I am going to open your graves and lift you out of your graves, O My people, and bring you to the land of Israel."[6]

The prediction of Ezekiel 37 was fulfilled, said Netanyahu. I thought of Ron Nachman, the man who saw the bones of his nation reconnect and rise. How he labored to breathe life into his nation. And I felt the sorrow of the day I received a call from Robert Mawire who told me he had the worst kind of news. The visionary mayor of Ariel had been diagnosed with an aggressive cancer.

Robert and I flew to Israel to pray with Ron. We had no agenda, nothing but friendship and God's leading. We arrived at his home to find him recovering from surgery and chemotherapy. We sat on the carpeted floor next to him, put our hands gently on his shoulders, and prayed. We cried out to God to comfort and heal him. Tears ran down our faces, and the Holy Spirit enveloped us in His embrace.

Months later Ron Nachman stood in front of my congregation with a wide smile, looking and sounding healthy and robust. "I feel like I'm home when I'm here," he said to enthusiastic applause. "First, thank you to all those families who hosted our children from Ariel. You can't know the impact it has for them to come here." He was referring to an exchange program we had developed for students from Ariel (more on that later).

He had much to say about his beloved city and nation and made his points to frequent applause. Then he quieted the room by saying, "Now I need to share something very personal. Unfortunately I got sick with cancer a year and a half ago." He talked about the time Robert and I visited. He said that he was touched by our visit and our prayers.

"Pastor Bentley and Robert Mawire prayed and then asked thousands of people to pray. So now, I am here, my first time in the United States after treatments, and I want to come to Maranatha Chapel and say thank you. I pray that God will give us many days to work together to overcome the difficulties we face."

I thought about the orchids he grew. He was proud of them and liked to show them off. "This hothouse is always blossoming and renewing," he once said. "It gives you hope for life, for the battle you are waging."[7]

I prayed that he would be with us in the decade to come. There are indeed battles to be waged.

What God's Signs in the Heavens Tell Us

WE ARE FAMILIAR WITH THE STORY OF JOB, A MAN
who was righteous in God's eyes but still suffered more on earth than anyone should
have to. At the end of the ordeal, after God had shown Satan that his servant Job
would remain faithful, Job asked God for an account. He wanted God to explain all
that had happened. It's understandable that a man who has been obedient to God
would wonder why so much suffering had befallen him.

Here is God's answer:

> Can you bind the cluster of the Pleiades,
> Or loose the belt of Orion?
> Can you bring out Mazzaroth in its season?
> Or can you guide the Great Bear with its cubs? (Job 38:31–32)

Most of us, after having gone through a prolonged ordeal, would not consider
that much of an explanation. By human standards it completely fails to answer the
question of undeserved suffering. But as God sees things, the statement makes perfect sense. He was challenging Job to open his eyes to a bigger reality than just his
life and circumstances. Today, God is challenging us to do the same.

In His answer to Job, the Lord referenced several well-known constellations,
but He also referred to Mazzaroth. That is not a word we hear often, and I have

wondered why it is included. I received an answer from Bible teacher Mark Biltz. He said it is the zodiac. *Strong's Concordance* also defines Mazzaroth as "the 12 signs of the Zodiac and their 36 associated constellations."[1]

Biltz had been doing research on lunar eclipses, using data he obtained from the National Aeronautics and Space Administration (NASA). He correlated the dates of eclipses from premodern times with events in the Bible (we will explore that in detail in a later chapter). As part of that research, he discovered something none of us would have expected—a connection between the zodiac and the gospel.

Deeper Meanings in the Symbols of the Zodiac

God created the zodiac, Scripture says. He painted twelve signs in the night sky, standing out like jeweled hieroglyphics. Why would He do that?

For at least twenty-five hundred years after the Creation, there was no Bible, no Torah, no written revelation from God. He spoke to individuals (Adam and Eve, Abraham, Noah, Moses) on specific occasions. But how did He communicate to people who were not chosen to perform acts of faith and courage that we read about today? How would He have communicated to you and me had we been alive at that time? I believe He used signs that people would recognize.

At the dawn of the first light, God said, "Let there be lights in the firmament of the heavens to divide the day from the night; and let them be for signs and seasons" (Genesis 1:14). What "signs" was He referring to? The reference to signs in Genesis comes from the Hebrew *oth*, which means "signal" (literally and figuratively), a distinguishing mark or miracle, a remembrance, omen, banner, warning or proof.[2]

The signs in the stars were meant to point us to Jesus and His redemption of the human race. God wasted no time in declaring that Yeshua, the Lamb of God, was slain. He gave us that truth from the foundations of the world (see Revelation 13:8). The story was always there, and from the beginning, God put the story in the heavens where people would notice it and could read it.

When I first taught the book of Genesis as a young pastor, I relished in creation and was satisfied to know that God created heavenly lights to order the universe. But

I didn't realize that they have an even greater meaning and purpose: to communicate. To be God's Word before the written word.

Two books opened my eyes to the deeper meanings of creation and the universe. One is *The Witness of the Stars* by Anglican priest and scholar E. W. Bullinger in 1893. More recently, in 1989, the late D. James Kennedy, who was the senior pastor of Coral Ridge Presbyterian Church, wrote *The Real Meaning of the Zodiac.* From the histories of virtually all civilized nations, records exist of the major stars in a zodiac formation of twelve signs. Nearly all these records indicate that the twelve signs represent the same twelve things and in the same order.[3]

Ancient Persian and Arabian traditions credit the invention of astronomy to Adam, Seth, and Enoch.[4] Josephus, the ancient Jewish historian, also asserted that astronomy originated in the family of Seth. He wrote about Seth and his children: "They were also the inventors of that peculiar sort of wisdom which is concerned with the heavenly bodies, and their order."[5]

The Tower of Babel

Hundreds of years later, after the work of Seth and his children, Noah's descendants designed a city with a tower whose "top is in the heavens" (Genesis 11:4). Nothing in Scripture indicates the height of the tower. The ancients knew they couldn't build a tower that actually reached the stars, but they designed a planisphere—or star chart—as part of the tower. This addition pictured the signs of the twelve known constellations. The tower was an attempt to preserve and hand down to future generations the original revelation from God that was written in the heavens. But the construction project in Babel reinterpreted the message, reimagined its meaning, and removed God from His preeminent place in creation. Instead, the tower builders made humanity the center of the universe.

Bullinger makes a strong case for this view of Babel, tracing the history of astronomy from the pre-flood of Noah's era to the apostle Paul and beyond. The ancient Babylonians were accomplished stargazers. They perfected their calendar by studying the movements of the sun and moon and calculating eclipses. Works on astronomy occupied a huge part of Babylonian libraries. Their observations were made from towers called ziggurats, similar to the tower of Babel, and their discoveries set the stage for the science of astronomy that was to follow.[6]

Antigonus of Macedonia, who ruled from 276 to 239 BC, commissioned the poet Aratus, a native of Tarsus, to write "Phaenomena," a poem about the zodiac. Aratus also wrote "Diosemeia" (The Divine Sign), a second poem. Centuries later, in Athens, Paul discussed philosophy and theology with several Greeks at Mars Hill. In speaking of the Unknown God, Paul quoted "Phaenomena": "For in Him we live and move and have our being, as also some of your own poets have said, 'For we are also his offspring [children]'" (Acts 17:28).[7]

Stories of the zodiac filled the ancient world. But as astronomy mixed with astrology, the corruption of thought that began at the Tower of Babel shifted the focus from the Creator to creation, causing prophets such as Isaiah to warn:

> Let your astrologers come forward,
> those stargazers who make predictions month by month,
> let them save you from what is coming upon you.
> Surely they are like stubble;
> the fire will burn them up.
> They cannot even save themselves
> from the power of the flame.
> Here are no coals to warm anyone;
> here is no fire to sit by. (Isaiah 47:13–14, NIV)

Astrology is practiced by occultists who worship the stars; however, biblical astronomy is the study of the heavens and the interpretations of signs found in the stars that point us to Jesus Christ. According to Arabic tradition, the zodiac signs and the story of redemption came from Seth and Enoch, son and grandson of Adam. Both were men of faith and founders of this ancient understanding of the heavens.[8]

This perspective is foreign to what most of us have been taught. Critics of the reliability and accuracy of Scripture like to point out that many narratives in the Old

Testament supposedly borrowed from myths and legends of ancient Near Eastern cultures. But based on the research of Bullinger, Kennedy, and others, it appears likely that Gentile and pagan cultures were recasting and corrupting narratives and signs that began at the time of Creation and later with God's people, the Hebrews.

Biltz pointed out the obvious: God signaled the arrival of the Messiah with a star. And even this heavenly sign was prophesied more than fifteen hundred years before the birth of Christ. Balaam prophesied to the Israelites: "I see Him, but not now; I behold Him, but not near; a Star shall come out of Jacob; a Scepter shall rise out of Israel" (Numbers 24:17). Balaam's prophecy was fulfilled when the star of Bethlehem guided the Magi to the Messiah.

Rather than allow astrologers to corrupt the zodiac for their own purposes, it's important for Christians to gain an accurate understanding of the signs that God designed into the heavens and to know why He did so. Let's take a close look at the constellations as well as the twelve signs of the zodiac to discern what God is telling us.

Mazzaroth

The Mazzaroth is a timekeeper. The English word for Mazzaroth is *zodiac*, from the primitive Hebrew root word *sodi*, which in Sanskrit means a "way or step." Variations of this word, such as *sod*, carry the connotation of "secret," which reminds me of Deuteronomy 29:29: "The secret things belong to the LORD our God, but those things which are revealed belong to us and to our children forever, that we may do all the words of this law."[9]

As D. James Kennedy explained, if you paint a picture of the sky on a ceiling, you would have a 360-degree circle called an *ecliptic*. The ecliptic is divided into twelve houses—or mansions or tabernacles—of the sun. On the ecliptic are twelve major constellations or star pictures, each conveying a sign.

Twelve is a highly symbolic number in God's revelations. There are twelve constellations, twelve signs, twelve tribes of Israel, twelve apostles. Twelve represents perfection of government.

Imagine Adam looking to the heavens, wondering, listening to a voice in the wind as the Creator drew pictures in the stars, teaching him their significance. Here is a lion, a woman, a crab. There is a man running with a sword in one hand and a club in another, an archer, scales. He continued until He had shown Adam twelve pictures, each one a chapter in the story of salvation. Imagine Adam telling his son Seth, "These are not just stars, but God is telling us a story with these heavenly pictures."

This is the story of hope passed from generation to generation. The gospel was written in the stars. As the lives of the patriarchs unfolded, God was taking the stories He already had told through creation and was beginning to clarify and expand on the stories. This time He communicated the truths directly with the Israelites. God was transferring the pictures from the heavens to the earth.

Jacob had two wives, Leah and Rachel, and two concubines, Bilhah and Zilpah, and twelve sons, whose descendants became the twelve tribes of Israel. Each tribe bore one of the heavenly signs (Hebrew *oth*): "Everyone of the children of Israel shall camp by his own standard, beside the emblems of his father's house" (Numbers 2:2). This is not an isolated reference. Read Genesis 49, where Jacob blesses and describes his sons, and Deuteronomy 33, the blessing of Moses. You will see how each of the twelve tribes generated a story. There is a story and a particular meaning attached to each of the twelve tribes.

When Jacob and his family went to Egypt, "the children of Israel were fruitful and increased abundantly" (Exodus 1:7). They organized themselves according to their tribes. After wandering forty years in the desert, the tribes conquered the land of Canaan, where each tribe was allotted a territory.[10]

The tribes were divided into four groupings, arranged on four sides of the camp: north, south, east, and west. Four great signs marked each boundary of the camp and surrounded the tabernacle, home of the ark of the covenant, at the center of the camp. Not surprisingly, the zodiac has four sides corresponding to the four faces of the angelic cherubim described by Ezekiel: "As for the likeness of their faces, each had the face of a man; each of the four had the face of a lion on the right side, each of the four had the face of an ox on the left side, and each of the four had the face of an eagle" (1:10–11).

The early church fathers identified the parallels between the four faces of the cherubim and the four gospels. Matthew portrays the lion, emphasizing Jesus as Messiah and King of Israel. Mark, the Roman, gives us the ox, portraying the Messiah as the Servant of the Lord. Luke shows the face of a man, clarifying the humanity of the Messiah. And John reveals the eagle, a picture of the deity of Christ Jesus our Lord.

This study is not to be dismissed before it is carefully considered. God made these things clear to us from the first chapter of Genesis: "Let there be lights in the firmament of the heavens to divide the day from the night; and *let them be for signs and seasons,* and for days and years" (verse 14). And He revisited this idea in Scripture. Psalm 104 talks about the moon and sun marking the seasons. God made the lights in the sky to serve as timekeepers, to help humanity keep track of and communicate the times and seasons. But He also left us clues to help us discern the signs that He built into the heavenly constellations.

The Riddle of the Sphinx

THE HEBREWS NUMBERED SEVENTY WHEN JACOB'S family entered Egypt at Joseph's invitation to escape a severe famine. Some four hundred years later, when Moses delivered the Hebrew slaves from Egypt, they numbered around two million.

Though they escaped from Pharaoh and a harsh life of slavery, the Israelites left their mark on Egypt. The Jewish historian Josephus wrote of the Egyptians: "They became very abusive to the Israelites…they set them also to build pyramids."[1] We know Pharaoh forced the Hebrews into harsh labor, making bricks for the construction of his monuments: "You shall no longer give the people straw to make bricks as before…. And you shall lay on them the quota of bricks which they made before" (Exodus 5:7).

The work of the Hebrew slaves went far beyond gathering straw to use in building materials. The Israelites built the pyramids. And one of those ancient monuments—the Great Sphinx—holds the key to the Mazzaroth. The celebrated mystery and riddle of the Sphinx is really not so puzzling when you connect it to the zodiac. The people who built the famous monument held the ancient stories and knowledge from God in their hearts. The Sphinx answers a basic question: Where does the story of the zodiac begin, and where does it end?

The famous creature has the head of a woman and the body of a lion, and there the story begins to unfold. The constellation Virgo (the Virgin) foreshadows the promise of the Messiah born of a virgin. As we travel full circle around the zodiac, we end up at Leo (the lion), which is the climax of the story, the second coming of the Lion of the tribe of Judah. As we know, this is described in prophecy. The virgin and the lion, bookends of the gospel, are told in the stars. And in the Sphinx, the story is brought to earth in a desert monument that is celebrated and debated to this day.

D. James Kennedy points out: "In the Temple of Esneh in Egypt, there is a great sky painting in the portico on the ceiling which shows the whole picture of the zodiac. Between the figures of Virgo, The Virgin, and Leo, The Lion, there is carved the figure of the sphinx with the head of a woman and the body of a lion. The woman's face is looking at The Virgin and the lion's tail is pointing to Leo, telling us that we begin with The Virgin and end with Leo."[2]

Think of the twelve constellations as twelve chapters in a book. Virgo is chapter 1. Each chapter reveals one of the major signs, but it also contains three smaller constellations, called decans. The decans further illustrate and explain the major sign. A total of forty-eight constellations, taken together, are patterns of stars that still bear the Hebrew and Arabic names given them eons ago. And the forty-eight groupings of heavenly light tell the story of our redemption.

The Twelve Signs of the Mazzaroth (Zodiac)

Let's take a journey through the Mazzaroth, starting with chapter 1, Virgo. I encourage you to study the details for yourself, reading one of the books I mentioned or doing your own research. There are multiple layers of meaning, and we can barely touch on them here.

The Sign of Virgo, the Virgin

Virgo corresponds to the tribe of Zebulun, a son of Leah, one of Jacob's wives.[3] Virgo the virgin, also called Bethulah (which means "virgin" in Hebrew), is the beginning of all prophecy and represents the promise of salvation and the defeat of evil.

And I will put enmity
Between you and the woman,
And between your seed and her Seed;
He shall bruise your head,
And you shall bruise His heel. (Genesis 3:15)

The sign of Virgo depicts a woman holding a branch in her right hand and ears of corn in her left. Jesus the Messiah, born of a virgin, is the righteous Branch of Isaiah 11:1. These two words are connected, especially in Latin, where Virgo means "a virgin" and virga means "a branch."[4]

Again and again the Hebrew prophets painted a symbolic picture of the Messiah as a branch:

- "I will raise to David a Branch of righteousness; a King shall reign and prosper, and execute judgment and righteousness in the earth" (Jeremiah 23:5).
- "Behold, I am bringing forth My Servant the BRANCH" (Zechariah 3:8).
- "Behold, the Man whose name is the BRANCH! From His place He shall branch out, and He shall build the temple of the LORD" (Zechariah 6:12).
- "In that day the Branch of the LORD shall be beautiful and glorious" (Isaiah 4:2).

Virgo, the first chapter of this starlit story, announces that a virgin will bring forth the incarnation of God in the Messiah. He will be the Branch, the tree of life who will one day proclaim: "I am the vine, you are the branches. He who abides in Me, and I in him, bears much fruit" (John 15:5).

The Sign of Libra, the Scales

Libra corresponds to the tribe of Levi, a son of Leah. The Hebrew name for Libra is *Mozanaim,* meaning "the scales, weighing"; the Arabic version, *Al Zebuna,* means "purchase" or "redemption." The name by which it has come down to us is Latin—Libra, which means "weighing."

The prophets proclaimed what Libra teaches: "Who has measured the waters in the hollow of His hand, measured heaven with a span and calculated the dust of the earth in a measure? Weighed the mountains in scales and the hills in a balance?" (Isaiah 40:12).

When Daniel was brought before Belshazzar to read the handwriting on the wall, which spoke of weighing and measuring, he summarized the message with these words: "You have been weighed in the balances, and found wanting" (Daniel 5:27). We, too, have been weighed, we were found wanting, and we are separated from God by our sins, Libra cries. But other stars in this constellation were given names that tell the story of redemption: "The Price Deficient," "The Price That Covers," and "The Price of Conflict."

In the first decan (one of the three divisions of 10° within a sign of the zodiac) of the Libra chapter, the constellation named the Southern Cross resides, appearing and disappearing at different times and centuries. A beloved sign now seen in the Southern Hemisphere, it is the symbol for the cross that balances the scales!

The Sign of Scorpio, the Scorpion (or Serpens)

Scorpio corresponds with the tribe of Dan, a son of Bilhah. A giant scorpion attempts to sting the heel of a mighty man who grinds his heel into the scorpion's heart while wrestling with a serpent. Conflict in the heavens! The Hebrew and Arabic name for scorpion is *akrab*, which also means "conflict" or "war." Some Arabic interpretations connote "wounding him that comes."[5]

In Scripture a pattern emerges of Satan repeatedly trying to destroy the seed of Abraham—and failing.

- Haman, in the book of Esther, nurtured such a fanatical hatred of the Jews that he plotted to kill all the Jews in ancient Persia.
- Herod so feared and hated the virgin's son that he murdered all the baby boys in Bethlehem (see Matthew 2:16–18).

- Satan tempted Jesus in the wilderness, trying to lure Him into sin (see Mark 1:12–13; Matthew 4:1–11; Luke 4:1–13).
- In the Garden of Gethsemane, Jesus suffered the "hour, and the power of darkness" (Luke 22:53).

The pattern continued as the raging hatred boiled to the surface again and again through the Inquisition, the Ku Klux Klan, pogroms, Nazism, Islamic jihadists, and numerous other forms of anti-Semitism.

On the cross Jesus was wounded in the heel. There, the "scorpion" or "serpent" struck the woman's seed. When Jesus died and rose from the dead, He destroyed the works of the devil forever. Hallelujah!

The Sign of Sagittarius, the Archer

Sagittarius corresponds with the tribe of Asher, a son of Zilpah. His bow is aimed directly at the heart of the scorpion. Sagittarius, or the Archer, is a mirror of the Lord who will soon come, full of glory and honor and power, piercing all the King's enemies with His arrows. "Let your sharp arrows pierce the hearts of the king's enemies; let the nations fall beneath your feet," declared the psalmist (Psalm 45:5, NIV).

The Messiah's triumph was foreshadowed in the star picture called by the Latin name *Sagittarius,* meaning the archer. The Hebrew and Syriac names of the sign are *Kesith,* which means "the archer"; the Arabic name is *Al Kaus,* "the arrow."[6]

Three of the brightest stars in the constellation are named Naim (Hebrew: "The Gracious One"), Lyra ("Praise for the Conqueror"), and Vega, ("He Shall Be Exalted"). Jesus fits each of the descriptions. He is the Archer whose heel was stung by the scorpion, but His arrow pierces the scorpion's heart, forever vanquishing him.

The Sign of Capricorn, the Goat or Sea Goat

Capricorn corresponds with the tribe of Naphtali, a son of Bilhah. Sacrifice is the subject of Capricorn the Goat. Ancient zodiacs or planispheres depict a goat with a fish tail. The goat symbolizes atoning sacrifice, and the fish represents the people for whom the atonement is made. Capricorn pictures the goat as bowing his head, its right leg folded beneath its body, as if it is dying, unable to rise. But the tail of the fish is full of vigor and life. The goat sacrifices its life for the fish.

The goat is the animal used for the sin offering in Scripture: "Then say to the Israelites: 'Take a male goat for a sin offering'" (Leviticus 9:3, NIV; see also 10:16; 16:9–10). The Hebrew name of the sign is *Gedi,* which means "the kid" (that is, a young goat) or "cut off." The modern name comes to us from Latin, *Capricornus,* which also means "goat."

In Leviticus 16:7–10, two goats were presented as sin offerings: one to be sacrificed as an atonement (covering) for sin, and the other, called the scapegoat, was released into the wilderness. As the latter goat disappeared, symbolically the sins of the nation disappeared from sight. Every year this sacrifice was offered on the Day of Atonement, Yom Kippur.

Isaiah prophesied about the coming Messiah: "He was wounded for our transgressions, He was bruised for our iniquities; the chastisement for our peace was upon Him, and by His stripes we are healed" (53:5). The death of Christ on the cross perfectly fulfilled this promise. Jesus became our sacrifice, immersed into the waters of death yet coming alive in the resurrection. The tail of the fish is a symbol of life and blessing. In the miracles of Jesus and the multiplying of loaves and fishes, we see the multiplying of the redeemed.

The Sign of Aquarius, the Water Bearer

Aquarius corresponds with the tribe of Reuben (the Man), a son of Leah. While Capricorn shines brightly with the revelation of atonement, Aquarius depicts our Redeemer pouring out His Spirit upon us. Aquarius depicts a man pouring an inexhaustible supply of water from an urn into the mouth of a fish. The Hebrew name for this sign is *Deli,* the "water urn" or "bucket." Aquarius is the Latin name, which means "water pourer."

The Bible abounds with allusions to the Lord pouring out His Spirit—as water is poured out—upon His people. Jesus promised: "If anyone thirsts, let him come to Me and drink. He who believes in Me, as the Scripture has said, out of his heart will flow rivers of living water" (John 7:37–38).

Water is a promise of life:

- "For the earth shall be full of the knowledge of the LORD as the waters cover the sea," wrote Isaiah (11:9). See also Habakkuk 2:14.
- "There the majestic LORD will be for us a place of broad rivers and streams" (Isaiah 33:21).
- "I will sprinkle clean water on you, and you shall be clean" (Ezekiel 36:25).

The story of the water bearer is the story of the Savior giving a world the greatest substance of life; as fish need water, so we need the Spirit of the Lord. Jesus came not only to be our atonement but also to pour out life in a stream that never runs dry.

The Sign of Pisces, the Fishes

Pisces corresponds with the tribe of Simeon, a son of Leah. Pisces portrays two large fish bound together with bands around each tail. The Hebrew word *Dagim* means "the fishes." It is closely related to the concept of multitudes. In the beginning God told Adam and Eve to "be fruitful and multiply" (Genesis 1:28). He later promised Abraham that he would be the father to a multitude of descendants: "Look now toward heaven, and count the stars.... So shall your descendants be" (Genesis 15:5). The generations of Abraham continued to multiply, even in the bondage of Egypt.

One miracle is recorded in each of the four gospels: Jesus multiplying five loaves and two fish to feed more than five thousand people—with food left over (see Matthew 14:31–21; Mark 6:31–44; Luke 9:10–17; John 6:5–15). Pisces the fish is a symbol of Israel and of the early church. Persecuted Christians secretly drew half a fish in the sand as a secret sign; the other half was to be completed by another person. It was a way for Christians to identify themselves to each other.

In the New Covenant the apostle Paul wrote,

For he himself is our peace, who has made the two one and has destroyed the barrier, the dividing wall of hostility, by abolishing in his flesh the law with its commandments and regulations. His purpose was to create in himself one new man out of the two, thus making peace, and in this one body to reconcile both of them to God through the cross, by which he put to death their hostility. (Ephesians 2:14–16, NIV)

Multiplying and blessing. Jew and Gentile. Of the two, He makes one. Pisces is a clear picture of the heart of the Father and the heart of the Son.

The Sign of Aries, the Ram or Lamb

Aries corresponds with the tribe of Gad, a son of Zilpah. Aries is a lamb bounding across the night sky. Its Hebrew name is *Taleh,* "the lamb." The constellation's brightest star is called in Arabic *ras al-hamal,* meaning "the head of the ram." *Aries* is the Latin word for ram. The ram and the lamb are powerful symbols of salvation in Scripture:

- Jesus is "the Lamb slain from the foundation of the world" (Revelation 13:8).
- On Mount Moriah, as Abraham lifted his knife over his son Isaac, he was stopped by an angel, and he noticed a ram caught in a nearby thicket (Genesis 22:13).
- "Behold! The Lamb of God who takes away the sin of the world!" exclaimed John the Baptist (John 1:29).
- The Savior who gave His life for us declared, "I am the good shepherd. The good shepherd lays down his life for the sheep" (John 10:11, NIV).

Aries tells the story of the Lamb from heaven. In the book of Revelation, John is found weeping because no one is worthy to open the scroll with seven seals. "Behold, the Lion of the tribe of Judah, the Root of David!" one of the elders cried (5:5). But when John turned, he did not see a lion. He saw "a Lamb as though it had been slain" (verse 6).

John saw Jesus, the Lamb of God. And then he heard "the voice of many angels…, the living creatures, and the elders" numbering "ten thousand times ten thousand, and thousands of thousands," and they all sang, "Worthy is the Lamb who was slain to receive power and riches and wisdom, and strength and honor and glory and blessing!" (verses 11–12).

So far in our journey around the zodiac, from Virgo to Aries, we have watched the story of Jesus's first coming in humility and sacrifice. Now we turn to the story of His return as we anticipate the arrival of the King, the Lion of the tribe of Judah.

The Zodiac and Christ's Second Coming

ALL PROPHECY POINTS TO JESUS IN SOME WAY. MANY of the prophets saw detailed visions of the fulfillment of God's promise to send Israel a Messiah. In those prophecies we often see a second prophecy revealing the return, or second coming, of the Messiah.

God uses a variety of ways to reveal His love and His plans to humanity. Paul makes it clear in Romans 1:18–21 that even those who have not had a chance to hear the gospel are still without excuse, because God has revealed His power and glory through creation. God uses such unexpected things as constellations, symbols of the zodiac, and even the labor of the Hebrews when they were slaves in Egypt, building pyramids and monuments such as the Sphinx. Let's look at the ways God has revealed the second coming of His Son in the signs of the zodiac.[1]

The Sign of Taurus, the Bull

Taurus corresponds to Joseph's two sons, Ephraim and Manasseh (two horns of the bull), sons of Rachael (Joseph's mother) through Asenath (Joseph's wife). Some believe this is explained in Joshua 17:17: "Joshua said to the house of Joseph—to Ephraim and Manasseh—'You are numerous and very powerful. You will have not only one allotment'" (NIV).

The Latin word *taurus* in Arabic is *Al Thaur;* both mean bull. The Hebrew word is *Shur,* whose root means "coming" and "ruling." Taurus dazzles the skies with a picture of a ferocious rushing bull, head down, ready to explode into his enemies. This is a picture of the sacrificial Lamb, who becomes the charging bull, who will personally deliver the kingdom on earth as it is in heaven. The bull is a personification of judgment as well as a picture of Christ's coming to conquer and to rule.

> For the indignation of the LORD is against all nations,...
>
> "The wild oxen shall come down with them,
> And the young bulls with the mighty bulls;
> Their land shall be soaked with blood,
> And their dust saturated with fatness."
>
> For it is the day of the LORD's vengeance,
> The year of recompense for the cause of Zion.
> (Isaiah 34:2, 7–8)

Riding on the neck of the starry bull is a cluster of seven stars named the Pleiades, meaning "congregation of the judge or ruler." The word *Pleiades* comes to us through the Septuagint (the Greek translation of the Scriptures). The Hebrew name is *Kimah,* which means "heap." Pleiades is the star picture spoken of by the Lord in the book of Job and later in Amos (see Job 9:9; 38:31–32; Amos 5:8).

The seven stars represent the bride of Christ (the church) riding upon the neck of the Messiah. Early church fathers saw the seven stars as the seven churches in the book of Revelation—and those churches are situated near the Taurus Mountains. The brightest of the stars is called in Arabic *Al Cyone,* meaning "the center." In ancient times astronomers believed Pleiades to be the center of the universe. The Syriac translation for Pleiades is *Succoth,* meaning "booths." The Jewish Feast of Booths is a picture of God's dwelling in the midst of His people. After rendering judgment, God binds and heals.

The Sign of Gemini, the Twins

Gemini corresponds to the tribe of Benjamin, son of Rachael. The Hebrew name of this sign is *Thaumim,* which means "to be complete, coupled together, united, or twinned." When the apostle Paul left the island of Malta, he set "out to sea in a ship that had wintered in the island. It was an Alexandrian ship with the figurehead of the twin gods Castor and Pollux" (Acts 28:11, NIV). I had read that statement many times but never realized that Castor and Pollux (sometimes linked with Apollo and Hercules in mythology) are the twins of the tenth sign of the zodiac: Gemini.

Ancient zodiac pictures show two figures walking toward us. The figure on the left is casually holding a club; the other is holding a bow and arrow in one hand and a lyre or harp in the other.

The two brightest stars in Gemini are Castor, or Apollo, which means "ruler or judge," and Pollux, or Hercules, which means "the strong one coming to labor or suffer." Gemini is a revelation of the dual nature of Jesus: both God and man, Savior and Suffering Servant, King and Priest, deity united with humanity. We see His twofold work of suffering and glory and His twofold coming in humility and triumph. And we see an answer to the Savior's prayer:

> O Father, glorify Me together with Yourself.... [T]hat they all may be one, as You, Father, are in Me, and I in You; that they also may be one in Us, that the world may believe that You sent Me. And the glory which You gave Me I have given them, that they may be one just as We are one. (John 17:5, 21–22)

The Sign of Cancer, the Crab

Cancer corresponds to the tribe of Issachar, son of Leah. The Greek name for Cancer is *Karkinos,* which means "holding" or "encircling." The Latin word *Cancer* became the commonly used name for the sign. This sign appears next to last, just ahead of the grand finale: Leo the Lion. As we circle the zodiac, we arrive at the sign of the Crab, a unique portrait of the coming King and His Kingdom.

Crabs grow by exchanging smaller shells for larger ones, weaker bodies for stronger ones. Believers relate this to the resurrection, when we shall lay aside "this body of death" (Romans 7:24). A crab lives in two worlds: under water and on dry land. Similarly, a believer lives simultaneously in two worlds: heaven and earth. "Even though our outward man is perishing, yet the inward man is being renewed day by day," the apostle encourages us (2 Corinthians 4:16).

The crab has many legs (or members). Similarly, the body of Christ is made up of members from every kindred, tribe, and nation—yet all are one body (see 1 Corinthians 12:12–14). The crab's two main arms are for grasping and holding tightly. These have parallels in the biblical admonitions to "hold fast what is good" (1 Thessalonians 5:21) and to "lay hold of the hope set before us" (Hebrews 6:18). Paul encouraged Timothy to "fight the good fight of faith, lay hold on eternal life, to which you were also called and have confessed the good confession in the presence of many witnesses" (1 Timothy 6:12). The crab symbolizes the redeemed who have laid hold of eternal life.

Within the constellation of the Crab are two stars named northern donkey colt and southern donkey colt. The Crab is connected to the tribe of Issachar, whose tribal standard portrayed two donkeys, reflecting what Jacob told his sons:

Gather together, that I may tell you what shall befall you in the last days:...

Binding his donkey to the vine,
And his donkey's colt to the choice vine,
He washed his garments in wine,
And his clothes in the blood of grapes....

Issachar is a strong donkey,
Lying down between two burdens;
He saw that rest was good,
And that the land was pleasant;
He bowed his shoulder to bear a burden,
And became a band of slaves. (Genesis 49:1, 11, 14–15)

Jesus is our true Issachar. He has shouldered our unbearable burden. He has ushered us into rest and into a land that is pleasant. He encircles us. He is our eternal home, both now and forever.

The Sign of Leo, the Lion

Leo corresponds to the tribe of Judah, son of Leah. Our journey has come full circle. The word *paradise* means "a garden enclosed." The story of the Mazzaroth, arranged in a circle of twelve signs, encloses paradise. We began with Virgo and now close with the twelfth and last sign: Leo, the Lion of Judah. The Lion, of course, is the Messiah, King of kings and Lord of lords. Even as this completes the twelve signs of the zodiac, the riddle of the Sphinx is solved: between Virgo and Leo is the grand story of salvation.

The Hebrew name for Leo is *Arieh,* which means "the Lion." The brightest star in the constellation is Regulus, whose ancient meaning was "treading underfoot." Regulus is also Latin for "prince" or "little king." The Arabic translates it as "the heart of the lion." Several words in Hebrew mean lion, but this one means "a lion hunting its prey."

The standard of the tribe of Judah depicted a lion. When Jacob, whose name was changed to Israel, lay dying, he gave his final blessing to Judah: "Judah is a lion's whelp.... He bows down, he lies down as a lion; and as a lion, who shall rouse him?" (Genesis 49:9). The Messiah is called "the Lion of the tribe of Judah, the Root of David" (Revelation 5:5).

In the book of Revelation, we see John despairing because no one was worthy to open "the scroll" (5:1–4) until one of the elders said, "Do not weep. Behold, the Lion of the tribe of Judah" (verse 5).

The scroll, many believe, is the title deed to earth, forfeited by Adam[2]—until our Hero comes to our rescue. This sacred scroll contains the only means for the human race to recover what was lost, the only way back into paradise, the only way for men and women made in the image of God to be *fully restored.*

The cost of restoration is the life and blood of the Hero from heaven.

You are worthy to take the scroll,

And to open its seals;

For You were slain,

And have redeemed us to God by Your blood. (Revelation 5:9)

In Revelation, the opening of the seven seals unleashes the Day of the Lord, when the Lion comes with great power, violence, and force to destroy His enemies. There will be no mercy. When a lion's roar thunders, its enemies shake. So shall it be when the Lion of Judah opens the seals of the scroll.

The Messiah is both the Lion and the Lamb; within His character dwells the capacity for retribution against those who threaten His children. We are rapidly moving toward that final hour, when the Lion will be roused. We anticipate His return to earth. It has become a fire in my bones. The Hebrew prophet Hosea gives a graphic picture of what is coming:

So I will be to them like a lion;

Like a leopard by the road I will lurk;

I will meet them like a bear deprived of her cubs;

I will tear open their rib cage,

And there I will devour them like a lion.

The wild beast shall tear them. (Hosea 13:7–8)

In the Leo constellation the Lion's feet are about to descend upon and destroy Hydra, the great serpent. When the Lion defeats evil for the last time, the garden will be restored by the return of the conquering Messiah.

We have come full circle. The glory and peace of heaven will heal our world. The deserts will bloom, the rivers flow. The eyes of the blind will be opened, and the ears of the deaf unstopped. The lion will lie down with the lamb, and the governments of this world will fall where they belong: on the beautiful and broad shoulders of the Lion Messiah, Jesus Christ (see Revelation 19; Isaiah 35).

God said of the lights in the sky, "Let them be for signs and seasons" (Genesis

1:14). I was beginning to understand the signs, but now I am learning that seasons mean more than spring, summer, fall, and winter. Remember this principle of biblical interpretation: first the natural, then the spiritual. God's creation helps open our eyes to the deep spiritual truths of God's love, His kingdom, and His will, which is being revealed on earth. The seasons themselves are rich with revelations of the coming Messiah.

How Seasons and Feasts Reveal Christ's Second Coming

THOSE WHO STUDY THE ANCIENT HEBREWS FIND much in their worship, their experiences with God, and their religious practices and rituals that is of great value. Christians gain a clearer understanding of Scripture when they study such things as the courts and holy places within the temple, the laws regarding sacrifices, and the utensils used in temple observances.

However, we have missed the prophetic significance found in Hebrew feasts and festivals, many of which continue to be observed by Jews today. It is important to understand the history and origins of each feast and festival observance, but in doing such a study, don't overlook the prophetic signs and revelations contained in the observances.

God promised to send a Messiah, and He fulfilled that promise when Jesus Christ came to earth. The world was given the opportunity to receive the promised Messiah. Jesus returned to the Father, but the prophets made clear that the Messiah would return to earth. When this age draws to a close, the Messiah will come again.

God does not want humanity to miss His Son. He painted images of Christ and His work on an astounding variety of canvases. We have discussed the people of Israel, today's brothers and sisters of Jesus, rebuilding the Holy Land. We have talked about prophecy in Scripture—the words of the Hebrew prophets of ancient times. We have looked at the heavens for pictures of the salvation story in constellations and the stories they tell. All prophecy, whether from Isaiah, Ezekiel, or a less-widely known source, points to Jesus Christ.

The gift of salvation, paid for by Christ's death and revealed in power in Christ's resurrection, gives meaning to all that God is doing and soon will be doing on earth. There is a deeper meaning to be found in the Jewish calendar and its peculiar way of identifying the seasons of the year. The seasons specified in this calendar coincide with appointed feasts, specified by God as feasts of the Lord. The calendar, the seasons, and the feasts all help to open our eyes to aspects of the return of Christ.

As we look at seasons and festivals, we will once again enlarge our understanding of the ways God opens our eyes to the future He has planned for us. In getting to know God's heart through the various pictures He has painted, we can see much more clearly the future of His work and His will on earth.

In this chapter we will look at the spring feasts of the Jewish year. It is these feasts that point to the first coming of the Messiah. The spring feasts reveal details about His life, His suffering, and His death for the redemption of humanity.

The Feasts of the Lord

The congregation at my church in San Diego values the patterns of worship and the symbolism of ancient Jewish festivals and feasts. At times, as indicated on the Jewish calendar, we join in celebration by enacting an observance that dates back to the days of Moses. At the most recent celebration of the Feast of Trumpets, a thousand small horns trumpeted joyful sounds as the congregation danced in the courtyard. The aroma of Middle Eastern food wafted through the air. The sound of a large ram's horn (a shofar) echoed from the stage. We were connecting on a deep level with the Jewish roots of our faith.

I have noticed that participation in the Feast of Trumpets has grown every year. It seems to evoke a passionate desire to praise and sing—and dance!—before the

Lord. Jews from the area also have started attending. I see a bridge forming across that wide chasm.

How did this happen? When Bible teacher Mark Biltz challenged me with a teaching on the Jewish feasts, he said, "You know, these are not [exclusively] Jewish holidays. They weren't intended for the Jewish people alone. They're called the feasts of the Lord, so if you belong to the Lord, the feasts are for you."

I dug into the Scriptures to become more familiar with the feasts of the Lord. I read these words: "And the LORD spoke to Moses, saying, 'Speak to the children of Israel, and say to them: "The feasts of the LORD, which you shall proclaim to be holy convocations, these are My feasts"'" (Leviticus 23:1–2).

The word *feasts* in Hebrew is *moed,* meaning a "divine appointment" and "a signal, appointed beforehand."[1] The Hebrew word for *convocation* is *miqra,* which means "a public meeting or [dress] rehearsal."[2]

These feasts are divine appointments, with the timing of each adding to the greater meaning of the observance. "Each [feast] is part of a comprehensive whole. Collectively, they tell a story," wrote Marvin Rosenthal and Kevin Howard, co-authors of *The Feasts of the Lord.* "These feasts are also called 'holy convocations'; that is, they are intended to be times of meeting between God and man for 'holy purposes.' Since these seven feasts of the Lord are 'appointed times' for 'holy purposes,' they carry with them great sacredness and solemnity."[3]

In the West we think of the seasons as spring, summer, fall, and winter. In the Jewish culture the seasons are marked by the seven feasts of the Lord: Passover, Unleavened Bread, Firstfruits, Pentecost, Trumpets, the Day of Atonement, and Tabernacles. And according to the Hebrew language, they are dress rehearsals! That is what the apostle Paul meant when he wrote, "So don't let anyone condemn you for what you eat or drink, or for not celebrating certain holy days or new-moon ceremonies or Sabbaths. For these rules were only shadows of the real thing, Christ himself" (Colossians 2:16–17, NLT).

The feasts foreshadow the first and second comings of Jesus. The first four represent His first coming and the last three His second coming. They tell us the complete story of the Messiah and redemption. Let me show you how.

The Spring Feasts (Christ's First Coming)

The four spring feasts, celebrated for centuries before the Messiah's first advent, are Passover (*Pesach* in Hebrew), Unleavened Bread (*Hag Hamatzot*), Firstfruits (*Yom HaBikkurim*), and Pentecost (*Shavuot*). Each one rehearsed the passion of Jesus. They were prophetic in nature and served other purposes.

Jesus was crucified on the Feast of Passover; He was buried on the Feast of Unleavened Bread; He rose from the dead on the Feast of Firstfruits, and the Holy Spirit was poured out on the first believers on the Feast of Pentecost. Every major event of the Messiah's first coming occurred on the exact day of the corresponding Jewish feast.

Now we wait for the fulfillment of the fall feasts, the feasts that prophecy the Second Coming. The fall feasts are the Feast of Trumpets (*Yom Teruah*), the Feast of Atonement (*Yom Kippur*), and the Feast of Tabernacles (*Sukkot*). These are dress rehearsals for the Messiah's return to earth.

Following is an overview of the seven feasts and what they mean. Like our journey through the Mazzaroth, this overview only begins to peel back the layers of meaning and history found in each one. I hope this will give you an appetite to study more.

Passover (*Pesach*)

On the fourteenth day of the first month at twilight is the Lord's Passover. (Leviticus 23:5)

What really happened at Passover? Ten plagues were inflicted on the people of Egypt as Moses pleaded with Pharaoh, "Let My people go" (Exodus 9:1). When he knew what would happen in the tenth and final plague, Moses instructed the Hebrews to sacrifice an unblemished lamb and paint its blood on their doors and the beams above. Those who obeyed were "passed over" by the angel of death (Hebrews 11:28,

NLT), who came to claim the lives of firstborn sons. Since that night, Passover has been observed as a solemn memorial of the tragedy that forced Pharaoh's hand and gave God's people their freedom from slavery.

Almost fifteen hundred years later the feast of Passover was fulfilled by the sacrifice of the Messiah on a Roman cross.

As an observant and pious Jew, Jesus celebrated Passover by sharing His last supper with His disciples. They sang a hymn and walked to the Mount of Olives, where Jesus anticipated the suffering to come in an agonizing prayer in the Garden of Gethsemane (see Matthew 26:36–46). The next morning Jesus was crucified at the "third hour" (Mark 15:25; see also Psalm 22:14–16), which is nine o'clock.

Israel's morning and evening sacrifices were held at nine in the morning and three in the afternoon. Nine in the morning is when the priests offered up the Passover lamb. At the very moment the high priest was binding the Passover lamb to the altar in the temple, as the Jews had done for centuries (in a "dress rehearsal"), Roman soldiers were binding Jesus to the cross.

At three in the afternoon, when the high priest slaughtered the Passover lamb, Jesus died on the cross: "And when the sixth hour (about midday) had come, there was darkness over the whole land until the ninth hour (about three o'clock). And at the ninth hour Jesus cried with a loud voice, Eloi, Eloi, lama sabachthani?—which means, My God, My God, why have You forsaken Me [deserting Me and leaving Me helpless and abandoned]?" (Mark 15:33–34, AMP).

The Father had even planned the music for His Son's funeral. The observers of Passover always sang the Hallel (Psalms 113–118). Jews came from around the world to observe Passover, so the city of Jerusalem was crowded with residents as well as visitors from distant lands. Can you hear it? As the Son of God died, the hills and valleys resounded with thousands of Jewish voices:

> The stone which the builders rejected
> Has become the chief cornerstone.
> This was the LORD's doing;

It is marvelous in our eyes.

This is the day the LORD has made;

We will rejoice and be glad in it.…

God is the LORD,

And He has given us light. (Psalm 118:22–24, 27)

Just as the "chief cornerstone" was being rejected at Golgotha, the prophet Joel's prophecy was fulfilled: "The sun and the moon will grow dark, and the stars will diminish their brightness" (3:15). Supernatural darkness enveloped the land for three hours as Jesus died (see Mark 15:33).

Blood and Water Flow from the Temple's Side

Josephus reported that more than two million Jews visited Jerusalem for Passover in Jesus's time. A quarter of a million lambs would have been sacrificed at the temple.

Can you imagine? Each lamb's blood flowed upon the Temple Mount, splashing over the base of the altar. The priests were covered with blood, and to prevent the altar area from being flooded, the blood was channeled through a system of conduits to the lower levels. Meanwhile, some priests labored to bring water up from cisterns farther below in order to flood the bloody aqueducts that ran beneath the temple. More than sixty thousand gallons of blood flowed that day.

Because the temple faced east, a massive river of blood and water poured out of the right side of the Temple Mount, flooding Hinnom Valley, the "valley of blood." Try to picture this scene. Jesus is on the cross. At the same time, on the Temple Mount, blood and water flowed from the Passover lambs that were being sacrificed. Suddenly a Roman soldier's spear pierces Jesus's side. He is the perfect Lamb, the sinless sacrifice. And blood and water flow from His side. Israel's Passover ritual created a precise dress rehearsal for the crucifixion of the ultimate Passover Lamb.

When Jacob thought his son Joseph had died, he "tore his clothes" from top to bottom to express his broken heart (see Genesis 37:34). In the temple a curtain covered the entrance to the Holy of Holies. It was eighteen inches thick and woven with priceless threads of varied colors and gold. When Jesus gave up His Spirit, breathing His last on the cross, His Father tore that veil in the temple "from top to bottom" (see Matthew 27:51). The Father rent His garment, brokenhearted for His Son.

The Feast of Unleavened Bread (*Hag Hamatzot*)

And on the fifteenth day of the same month is the Feast of Unleavened Bread to the LORD; seven days you must eat unleavened bread. (Leviticus 23:6)

Jesus was buried on the day of the Feast of Unleavened Bread. This is the second feast, and it begins the day after Passover. It is named for the bread that is eaten. It is the seven-day Feast of Unleavened Bread. Leaven is the agent that causes fermentation, making bread rise. But all leaven is removed from Jewish households as a reminder of the Exodus from Egypt, when the Israelites fled in such haste that there was no time for bread to rise. They could not have leavened bread.

Leaven in the Bible represents sin or error. Jesus said, "Take heed and beware of the leaven of the Pharisees and the Sadducees" (Matthew 16:6). Later the apostle Paul warned the Christians in Corinth: "Therefore purge out the old leaven, that you may be a new lump, since you truly are unleavened. For indeed Christ, our Passover, was sacrificed for us. Therefore let us keep the feast, not with old leaven, nor with the leaven of malice and wickedness, but with the unleavened bread of sincerity and truth" (1 Corinthians 5:7–8).

To conform to Jewish custom, the body of Jesus was buried almost immediately after it was taken off the cross. It was placed in a borrowed tomb owned by Joseph of Arimathea. But Jesus's body did not decay, fulfilling the prophecy of Psalm 16:10: "For You will not leave my soul in Sheol, nor will You allow Your Holy One to see corruption."

Unleavened bread, or *matzah,* is a picture of Jesus's sinless body. "I am the bread of life," He said (John 6:35). Bethlehem, the city of His birth, means "house of bread."

Have you ever seen Jewish matzah? It is baked with stripes ("By His stripes we are healed" [Isaiah 53:5]) and punctured with tiny holes ("They will look on Me whom they pierced" [Zechariah 12:10]). The Passover ceremony consists of taking the middle matzah, breaking it, wrapping it in a cloth (burying it), hiding it, and later having it reappear (like a resurrection). Even in a modern Jewish Passover celebration, the gospel is clearly presented if we have eyes to see!

The Feast of Firstfruits (*Yom HaBikkurim*)

> When you come into the land which I give to you, and reap its harvest, then you shall bring a sheaf of the firstfruits of your harvest to the priest. He shall wave the sheaf before the LORD, to be accepted on your behalf. (Leviticus 23:10–11)

On the first day of the week after the Feast of Unleavened Bread, the Feast of Firstfruits marked the beginning of the grain harvests.

In Leviticus 23:10–11, the people are instructed to bring part of their earliest crops to the priest in the temple. These firstfruits were waved before the Lord in thankful worship. On this day, the Sunday following Passover, we celebrate the resurrection of Jesus. The word itself, *firstfruits,* implies there will be a second, future resurrection. This is what the apostle Paul meant when he said, "But each one in his own order: Christ the firstfruits, afterward those who are Christ's at His coming" (1 Corinthians 15:23). Jesus's resurrection is the fulfillment of the Feast of Firstfruits.

Pentecost (*Shavuot*)

> Count fifty days to the day after the seventh Sabbath; then you shall offer a new grain offering to the LORD. (Leviticus 23:16)

Before He ascended into heaven, Jesus promised His disciples, "You shall receive power when the Holy Spirit has come upon you" (Acts 1:8). This promise was fulfilled during the final spring feast: Shavuot, or Feast of Weeks, also called Pentecost because it is celebrated fifty days after the Feast of Firstfruits.

Shavuot was a pilgrim holiday, meaning that worshipers traveled from numerous countries to the temple. The apostles had come together to pray, and on the day of Pentecost, 120 disciples gathered in an upstairs room. Suddenly a rushing wind filled the house, followed by small eddies of fire alighting on their heads. They received the ability to speak in foreign tongues.

This is what the church remembers about Pentecost, but we forget (or don't know) that Pentecost has been celebrated by the Jewish people since the day Moses brought the Law down from Mount Sinai. Traditionally, Shavuot is commemorated by waving two loaves of bread before the Lord. Both loaves are baked with leaven, representing sinful man. The two loaves foreshadow the bride of Christ, the church, made up of Jews and Gentiles. The apostle Paul wrote, "For He Himself is our peace, who has made both one, and has broken down the middle wall of separation, having abolished in His flesh the enmity, that is, the law of commandments contained in ordinances, so as to create in Himself one new man from the two, thus making peace" (Ephesians 2:14–15).

In spite of eventually becoming predominantly Gentile, the church was founded and built by twelve Jewish apostles. Filled with the Holy Spirit on Pentecost, Peter, who had denied the Lord three times, preached with unbridled passion, quoting the prophet Joel:

> And it shall come to pass in the last days, says God,
> That I will pour out of My Spirit on all flesh;
> Your sons and your daughters shall prophesy,
> Your young men shall see visions,
> Your old men shall dream dreams....
> Before the coming of the great and awesome day of the LORD.
> And it shall come to pass

> That whoever calls on the name of the LORD
> Shall be saved. (Acts 2:17, 20–21)

No longer just a dress rehearsal, the Feast of Pentecost had been fulfilled! Three thousand souls were born again that Pentecost day, a number that holds great significance. Three thousand people died on the day Moses carried the Law down Mount Sinai because he found them, on that first Pentecost, worshiping a golden calf (see Exodus 32:1–28). The apostle Paul noted, "For the letter kills, but the Spirit gives life" (2 Corinthians 3:6).

Imagine the early church realizing that Jesus was crucified on Passover, buried on the Feast of Unleavened Bread, and resurrected on the day of Firstfruits. Multitudes had come to Jerusalem for Pentecost, then the first believers experienced the power of the Holy Spirit, which launched the church into new lands and people. I can picture them rolling up their sleeves, so to speak, filled with joy and expectation as the long summer harvest began.

Dress Rehearsals and the Real Thing

Dress rehearsals are prophecy. They are prophecy acted out, pictures of the future brought to life in the annual feasts—and in our sacred celebrations—Good Friday, Resurrection Day (Easter), and Pentecost. Those beautiful Jewish holidays are rich with tradition but also rich in meaning.

In prophetic terms the long summer harvest correlates to the church age. Christ's death and resurrection were followed by two thousand years of harvesting, as the "Lord added to the church daily those who were being saved" (Acts 2:47). And now we move into fall, the time when the promise of the fall feasts is waiting to be fulfilled. All three of the fall feasts occur in the seventh month of Israel's calendar. The seventh day and the seventh year were holy under Mosaic laws. *Tishri,* the seventh month, is also holy, seven being the biblical number for perfection and completion. Notice the following:

- After creation, God rested on the seventh day, establishing the Sabbath.
- The Lord ordained seven feasts to tell the story of redemption.
- The Lord commanded the nation of Israel to refrain from farming every seventh year to allow the land to rest (Shemittah Year; see Leviticus 25:4).
- Seven sevens of years (forty-nine) were followed by a Jubilee Year, when all debts were canceled and all slaves set free.
- In the book of Daniel, seventy sevens (four hundred and ninety years) were determined as the period during which God would complete redemption (see Daniel 9:24–27).
- The book of Revelation uses the number seven more than fifty times, including the seven seals, seven trumpets, and seven bowls.[4]

Now we will turn to the fall feasts that prophesy Christ's *second* coming. The fall feasts are the Feast of Trumpets (*Yom Teruah*), the Feast of Atonement (*Yom Kippur*), and the Feast of Tabernacles (*Sukkot*). These are exciting dress rehearsals that have the ability to open people's eyes and hearts to the Messiah's return to earth.

Prophetic Truth Found in the Fall Feasts of the Jewish Calendar

THE SPRING FEASTS WERE PROPHECIES COMMUNICATED through required religious observances, foretelling the fulfillment of God's promise to send a Messiah. For thousands of years the spring feasts of the Lord drove home the promise and its fulfillment: the Messiah is coming. Look for Him.

Now we will look at the fall feasts, observances that prophesy God's work still to come. Yet we anticipate them with great hope. As the Feast of Trumpets shows, the summer harvest will end with the sound of a trumpet. And with that sound, the fall feasts begin. These feasts of the Lord are vivid pictures of the events that the church eagerly awaits.

The Feast of Trumpets (*Yom Teruah*)

In the seventh month, on the first day of the month, you shall have a sabbath-rest, a memorial of blowing of trumpets, a holy convocation. (Leviticus 23:24)

The sound of a trumpet is a powerful and recurring symbol in Scripture. When the Lord instituted the Feast of Trumpets, He was letting us know that something significant would happen. The Feast of Trumpets is also called Rosh Hashanah (Yom Teruah in Hebrew). Teruah, traditionally understood as the blowing of a ram's horn, is also translated as joyful noise or sound, as in Psalm 89: "Blessed are the people who know the joyful sound!" (verse 15).

I love what Zola Levitt, a Jewish believer who is now with the Lord, wrote:

> The trumpet was the signal for the field workers to come into the Temple.
> The High Priest actually stood on the southwestern parapet of the Temple
> and blew the trumpet so that it could be heard in the surrounding fields. At
> that instant, the faithful would stop harvesting, even if there were more crops
> to bring in, and leave immediately for the worship services.[1]

The Feast of Trumpets foreshadows the end of an era and the rapture of the church:

> For the Lord Himself will descend from heaven with a shout, with the voice
> of an archangel, and with the *trumpet of God*. And the dead in Christ will rise
> first. Then we who are alive and remain shall be caught up together with
> them in the clouds to meet the Lord in the air. And thus we shall always be
> with the Lord. Therefore comfort one another with these words. (1 Thessalo-
> nians 4:16–18)

When that trumpet sounds, the greatest miracle since Jesus rose from the dead will take place:

> We shall not all sleep, but we shall all be changed—in a moment, in the
> twinkling of an eye, at the last trumpet. For the trumpet will sound, and the
> dead will be raised incorruptible, and we shall be changed. For this corrupt-
> ible must put on incorruption, and this mortal must put on immortality.
> (1 Corinthians 15:51–53)

Why the Feast of Trumpets Is Unique

The Feast of Trumpets is the only Jewish celebration that occurs on the first day of the month, at the new moon, when the moon is dark except for a thin crescent. All other Jewish holidays occur later in their respective months, when the moon is bright. In ancient Israel the new moon was normally celebrated by short trumpet blasts, but the New Moon of Tishri was celebrated by long trumpet blasts, signifying the uniqueness and sacredness of the seventh month.[2]

After the Diaspora, when Jews were scattered all over the world, Rosh Hashanah began to be celebrated over a two-day period so that the Jews living in different time zones could be included. They began to call it "one long day." The Feast of Trumpets became a mystery. *No one could say the exact day or hour it began.*

Blowing the Shofar

God instructed Moses to "make two silver trumpets for yourself;…you shall use them for calling the congregation and for directing the movement of the camps" (Numbers 10:2). By Solomon's time, 120 priests were sounding silver trumpets in the temple (see 2 Chronicles 5:12). But the shofar is the trumpet used for the Feast of Trumpets. The sound of the shofar carries memories for Jews of their origins and history.

When Abraham, in obedience to God, took his son Isaac to the top of Mount Moriah to offer him as a sacrifice, an angel held him back. A ram caught in the bushes became the substitute offering. That is why a ram's horn is a powerful reminder of Isaac's deliverance and Abraham's obedience—and how their story foreshadowed the sacrifice of our heavenly Father's own Son (see Genesis 22:10–14).

The ram's horn has since trumpeted momentous Jewish events from war to celebrations, from Joshua's victory at Jericho to "proclaim liberty throughout all the land to all its inhabitants" in the Year of Jubilee (Leviticus 25:10).

Perhaps one year very soon, on a Feast of Trumpets, the Lord will descend with a shout, blow the shofar of God, and take the church home in a glorious instant. And we will be spared as Isaac was!

The Next Event

The dress rehearsal known as the Feast of Trumpets is the next event to be fulfilled on the prophetic calendar. This feast tells us about the fulfillment of the ancient prophets' visions surrounding the rapture of the church. The trumpet is poised, ready to herald the end of the summer harvest.

Rosh Hashanah, which in Hebrew means "head of the year," is known by various Hebrew idioms in addition to the Feast of Trumpets: the Wedding of the Messiah, the Hidden Day, the Time of Jacob's Trouble, the Day of the Awakening Blast, the Day of Judgment, and the Coronation of the Messiah. Even these alternate names for the observance tell us something about this feast and what it means. Let's look at a few.

The Wedding of Messiah

"Blow the trumpet in Jerusalem!... [C]all the people together.... Call the bridegroom from his quarters and the bride from her private room" (Joel 2:15–16, NLT). A royal wedding is announced by the sound of trumpets, and the wedding is blessed under the traditional canopy.[3]

Marriages in ancient Israel were arranged by parents, like Abraham did for his son Isaac. Typically the bridegroom would go to the house of the bride-to-be (sometimes their first meeting) and bring three things: the wedding contract, a skin of wine, and the bride price. After the father approved the bride price, the young man would present his vows of love. A glass of wine would be poured, and the betrothal contract then became a legal document, a *ketubah*. The couple's status changed to betrothed, and they were legally married, though the wedding ceremony was still some time away.

With all the transactions completed, the groom took his betrothed aside to tell her that he was going away to build their bridal chamber. When the chamber was finished, he would return for her. Who decides when the chamber is ready? The groom tells his bride that he does not know exactly when the wedding will begin. Only his *father* determines the day and hour (see Mark 13:32).

This is when the bride begins the wait for the day when her groom will come to capture her. She is confident of his return for two reasons: the vows he pledged and the price he paid. Meanwhile, she wears a veil to signify that she is taken.

She receives regular progress reports about her new home. The foundation is laid. The walls are up. The doors are hung. Now the roof! Her excitement grows. Any day her beloved will come. She gathers her closest friends, and they begin watching through the night, two by two, waiting to hear the shouts of young men as they race toward her father's home (see Matthew 25:6–7). This gives her just minutes to wake up, ready to be "raptured" from her own home.

Traditionally the Jewish father waited until the middle of the night, when his son was fast asleep and tired from all his hard work. I can picture the proud father gently shaking his son and whispering, "It's time." Time to claim his bride.

When Jesus told His disciples, "If I go and prepare a place for you, I will come again and receive you to Myself" (John 14:3), He was giving the speech of a Jewish bridegroom. He paid the ultimate bride price. "Knowing that you were not redeemed with corruptible things, like silver or gold,...but with the precious blood of Christ, as of a lamb without blemish and without spot" (1 Peter 1:18–19).

He gave us our ketubah (our contract) through the promises in His Word, and He invites us to the most glorious wedding that will ever take place (Revelation 19:7–9). "Blessed are those who are called to the marriage supper of the Lamb!" (verse 9).

The Hidden Day

Because no one could know the exact day of Rosh Hashanah (remember, it was celebrated over a two-day period), it was also called the Hidden Day (*Yom HaKeseh*). The term *keseh* or *keceh* is derived from the Hebrew root *kacah*, which means "to conceal, cover, or hide."

When Jesus said, "No one knows about that day or hour" (Matthew 24:36, NIV), He meant the day of His return is unknown. But in another layer of meaning, to the Jewish mind, He was also using an idiom for Rosh Hashanah, the "hidden day."[4]

Four times in the New Testament we read, "I am coming as a thief," "I will come upon you as a thief, and you will not know what hour I will come upon you," "the day of the Lord will come as a thief in the night," "the day of the Lord so comes as a thief in the night" (Revelation 16:15; 3:3; 2 Peter 3:10; 1 Thessalonians 5:2). A thief does not arrive when you expect him. Instead, it's indefinite, just like a Jewish wedding! An unexpected arrival at an unknown time.

Alfred Edersheim, a nineteenth-century Jewish believer, wrote a number of wonderful books connecting the Scriptures to their Jewish background. In one he explained why the high priest was called a thief in the night. Originally, God supernaturally ignited the holy fire on the temple altar. Afterward, at least two priests were to constantly mind the flame to make sure it never went out. The high priest would occasionally make rounds during the night to ensure the priests had not fallen asleep. If they did, God forbid, the high priest would take fire from the altar and light the sleeping priests' garments; they would awaken with a fright, tearing their burning clothes off, exposing their nakedness.[5]

Now read Jesus's words: "Behold, I am coming as a thief. Blessed is he who watches, and keeps his garments, lest he walk naked and they see his shame" (Revelation 16:15). We do not know the day or hour of His return, but we can hold fast and tend the flame of our faith, that it may never die.

The Time of Jacob's Trouble

Remember that Rosh Hashanah falls in the darkest part of the lunar cycle. The fulfillment of the Feast of Trumpets sets the stage for the tribulation on earth, the Day of the Lord, when God's wrath will be poured out on Israel's enemies and the world will be brought to judgment.

Zephaniah and Amos described days of darkness and gloominess (Zephaniah 1:15; Amos 5:20). Further, the dark moon of Rosh Hashanah augurs Joel's prophecy:

> The sun shall be turned into darkness,
> And the moon into blood,

> Before the coming of the great and awesome day of the LORD.
> And it shall come to pass
> That whoever calls on the name of the LORD
> Shall be saved. (Joel 2:31–32)

Oh, the hope that last line gives! Judgment will bring redemption and a fulfillment of the Abrahamic Covenant when, as Paul prophesied, "All Israel will be saved" (Romans 11:26).

The Coronation of Messiah

The custom regarding new kings of Israel and Judah required that they be enthroned on the first day of Tishri, the seventh month—the Feast of Trumpets. This feast foreshadows the coronation of the Messiah. Daniel wrote, "I watched till thrones were put in place.… The court was seated, and the books were opened" (7:9–10). Judgment day had come, just as Rosh Hashanah warns. But look what follows:

> One like the Son of Man,
> Coming with the clouds of heaven!…
> Then to Him was given dominion and glory and a kingdom,
> That all peoples, nations, and languages should serve Him.
> (verses 13–14)

In Revelation 4:1–11, John described the ultimate coronation after judgment. He heard a voice "like a trumpet" just before he was taken up "in the Spirit" and brought before a throne illuminated by a rainbow of jewels and a crystal sea. The One who sat upon the throne shone like jasper and sardius. Four living creatures (the ones we met in the Mazzaroth with the faces of a lion, ox, eagle, and man) and twenty-four elders fell before Him, worshiping, casting their crowns, and giving glory and honor and thanks, saying:

You are worthy, O Lord,

To receive glory and honor and power;

For You created all things,

And by Your will they exist and were created.

(Revelation 4:11)

The Feast of Trumpets is the dress rehearsal for the glorious commencement of the kingdom of God on earth.

The Feast of Atonement (*Yom Kippur*)

Also the tenth day of this seventh month shall be the Day of Atonement. It shall be a holy convocation for you; you shall afflict your souls, and offer an offering made by fire to the LORD. (Leviticus 23:27)

Moses came down from Mount Sinai, his arms wrapped around two large clay tablets. He'd spent forty days in God's presence. Forty days on holy ground, receiving the Law, seeing the words miraculously inscribed on the tablets.

He must have been horrified to see the decadent, rebellious scene in the Hebrew camp. His people were dancing and worshiping a golden calf, indulging in food and drink. Furious, Moses threw the tablets down, smashing them into pieces. But in spite of his anger, Moses returned to the Lord to seek atonement for his people. He pleaded, "Forgive their sin—but if not, I pray, blot me out of Your book which You have written" (Exodus 32:32).

That dash between "forgive their sin" and "but if not" is a long pause, the like of which occurs nowhere else in Scripture. Understand what Moses was saying. He begged the Lord to forgive the people. But if not...

Moses's willingness to be stricken from God's book is a powerful foreshadowing of the sacrifice of Jesus and the story behind the Day of Atonement. This day, also known as Yom Kippur, is the sixth feast and occurs on the tenth day of Tishri, ten days after the Feast of Trumpets. *Kippur* is from the Hebrew word *kaphar,* meaning "to cover." This is the most sacred and solemn day in the Jewish year. It is designated as a day of confession, a day to "afflict your souls" (Leviticus 23:27). Prior to AD 70, the people fasted and repented while the high priest entered the Holy of Holies, first to make a sacrifice on his own behalf, and then on behalf of the nation (see Leviticus 16:1–34; 23:27). Today, the main focus of Yom Kippur centers around synagogue services, often decorated in white to symbolize purity and cleansing from transgression.[6]

The blood of bulls sacrificed on Yom Kippur covered sins. In contrast, the promised Messiah, Yeshua, took sins away forever: "He took blood into that Most Holy Place, but not the blood of goats and calves. He took his own blood, and with it he secured our salvation forever" (Hebrews 9:12, NLT).

The Day of Atonement will be fulfilled by the second coming of Jesus the Messiah, when He returns to establish His kingdom. It will be an emotional day for the Jewish people when they see their Messiah *and know him* for the first time:

> And I will pour on the house of David and on the inhabitants of Jerusalem the Spirit of grace and supplication; then they will look on Me whom they pierced. Yes, they will mourn for Him as one mourns for his only son, and grieve for Him as one grieves for a firstborn....
>
> In that day a fountain shall be opened for the house of David and for the inhabitants of Jerusalem, for sin and for uncleanness. (Zechariah 12:10; 13:1)

According to Zechariah 14:4–5, on that day, the Lord's feet will stand on the Mount of Olives, and the mount will be split from east to west, creating a large valley. Half the mountain will move north, half south, and people will run through the valley as if fleeing an earthquake. "Thus the LORD my God will come" (verse 5). Christ will touch down on the Mount of Olives for all to see. This is the day that "all Israel will be saved" (Romans 11:26).

The Feast of Tabernacles (*Sukkot*)

The fifteenth day of this seventh month shall be the Feast of Tabernacles for
seven days to the LORD. On the first day there shall be a holy convocation.
(Leviticus 23:34–35)

The trumpet has called us home. The Messiah returns and sits on the throne. What's
next? What God has always desired. God has intended all along to dwell or *tabernacle* with His people.

On the first Day of Atonement, the children of Israel wondered if they could be
forgiven—until Moses came down from the mountain after another forty days, his
face shining with God's glory. Atonement had been made. God declared His desire
to tabernacle among them: "And let them make Me a sanctuary, that I may dwell
among them. According to all that I show you, that is, the pattern of the tabernacle
and the pattern of all its furnishings, just so you shall make it" (Exodus 25:8–9).

The first Day of Atonement was the tenth day of the month Tishri. Overflowing
with joy and thanksgiving, the nation for the next five days gathered all the materials
needed to build the tabernacle, which would house the ark of the covenant and
God's divine presence. Moses asked those with willing hearts to bring an offering;
the people gave abundantly, beyond what was needed, until Moses had to ask them
to stop (see Exodus 36:6–7).

Each year during the Feast of Tabernacles, the fifteenth day of the seventh
month, the seventh full moon of the year, devout Jews build shelters outside their
homes in which to worship the Lord for seven days. They do this to remember that
God *tabernacled* among the people in the wilderness. Leviticus 23:39–40 describes
the feast: "Also on the fifteenth day of the seventh month, when you have gathered
in the fruit of the land, you shall keep the feast of the LORD for seven days; on the
first day there shall be a sabbath-rest, and on the eighth day a sabbath-rest. And you
shall take for yourselves on the first day the fruit of beautiful trees, branches of palm
trees, the boughs of leafy trees, and willows of the brook; and you shall rejoice before
the LORD your God for seven days."

God intended this feast to help future generations "know that I made the children of Israel dwell in booths when I brought them out of the land of Egypt: I am the LORD your God" (verse 43).

This last feast of the year, celebrated with great joy, was also called the Feast of Ingathering, because it was observed after all the crops had been harvested and gathered.[7]

Passover saw the barley harvest in the spring. Pentecost ushered in the summer harvest of wheat. The fall feasts encompassed the fruit harvests of grapes, pomegranates, and olives. This is recorded in the book of Revelation: "Thrust in your sharp sickle and gather the clusters of the vine of the earth, for her grapes are fully ripe" (14:18). The book of Revelation is actually about the fulfillment of the fall feasts. We cannot fully appreciate or understand Revelation without a knowledge of the fall feasts.

This harvest is both a time of judgment and of salvation. The tribulation described in the book of Revelation will see the greatest harvest of souls in history.

> After these things I looked, and behold, a great multitude which no one could
> number, of all nations, tribes, peoples, and tongues, standing before the
> throne and before the Lamb, clothed with white robes, with palm branches in
> their hands, and crying out with a loud voice, saying, "Salvation belongs to
> our God who sits on the throne, and to the Lamb!" (Revelation 7:9–10)

The Feast of Tabernacles is a dress rehearsal, anticipating and foreshadowing the day when the world can rejoice as the prophets foretold:

> And it shall come to pass that everyone who is left of all the nations which
> came against Jerusalem shall go up from year to year to worship the King,
> the LORD of hosts, and to keep the Feast of Tabernacles. (Zechariah 14:16)

> Behold, the tabernacle of God is with men, and He will dwell with them, and
> they shall be His people. (Revelation 21:3)

We see in the feast a prophecy of the thousand-year reign of the Messiah on earth. Now His Kingdom begins. Glorious!

The feasts are not a law for Christians. We are not obligated to observe them. But oh what we are missing! If you are invited to the dress rehearsal of a special event, you might want to attend if the practice will help you participate in a more meaningful way.

When Jesus comes again, He is coming for His bride, the church. He is planning the marriage supper of the Lamb in heaven (see Revelation 19:7–10). You don't want to miss the dress rehearsal—especially if you are in the wedding party.

The Feasts Still Open Our Eyes to God

THE FEASTS OF THE LORD, WHILE STILL OBSERVED by observant Jews, also coincide with events that shake the world. For instance, in 2008 on the day of the Feast of Trumpets, we heard a trumpet call that set off alarms around the world. The Dow Jones Industrial Average plunged 777 points, putting stock markets around the world under great stress. During that week of financial upset, we saw the beginning of a slide into economic decline that set the stage for what I call the Season of Destiny.

I consider the 2008 stock market crash an important signal. It was the beginning of a period of anxiety, uncertainty, and worldwide financial insecurity. I find the repeated occurrence of the number seven in the timing of this economic reversal interesting in view of its biblical significance.

Professor Nicholas Boyle, president of Magdalene College, Cambridge University, wrote a book titled *2014: How to Survive the Next World Crisis*. His theory is that every century is defined by what happens in the first twenty years. He believes another dramatic event will occur in 2014 or 2015 that will determine the course of this century. Over the last five hundred years, a cataclysmic event of international significance has occurred in the middle of the second decade of each century, sparking wars, religious conflict, or peace.[1]

"So what will be the great event that…will both symbolize and determine the character of the twenty-first century?" Boyle wrote. "It is likely that the present turmoil in world economics is leading up to that Great Event which will either re-solve the crisis of the next seven years or so or mark its catastrophic conclusion."[2]

Also, four significant celestial events—signals—have been predicted by NASA for 2014 and 2015. They involve the appearance of four blood moons (total lunar eclipses) on feast days. We will look at their importance in chapter 20.

Today, God Is Building an Ark

As it was in the days of Noah, so it will be also in the days of the Son of Man. (Luke 17:26)

God established a pattern with the story of the great flood and Noah's ark. In those events He gave us a striking example of first seeing the natural event and then the spiritual application. This is true of the prophetic revelations throughout Scripture.

Remember the earlier discussion of patterns? God establishes patterns of events to help us understand the past and the future. And the apostle Paul reiterated the principle in 1 Corinthians 15:46 that one of the most consistent divine patterns is the natural first and then the spiritual: "The spiritual is not first, but the natural, and afterward the spiritual." The account of Noah's ark is told in some form in almost every ancient culture's history and literature. This suggests that God wanted to warn not just the Jews, who would receive the Hebrew Scriptures, but also the Gentiles.

Noah's name in Hebrew means "rest" or "comfort." On the surface his life seemed far from restful or comfortable. He received a terrible word from the Lord, decrying the wickedness of humanity and vowing destruction of the earth. Noah and his family would be the exception. In a world filled with hatred and violence, he stood out as a "just man" who "walked with God" (Genesis 6:9).

He spent 120 years building an ark of gopher wood according to the specific instructions the Lord gave him. The ark's dimensions and design were mandated. There is no doubt that Noah was jeered, questioned, and ridiculed as he built this huge ship. When he warned the people of impending judgment, they likely saw nothing more than a victim of deception or possibly a madman. But Noah's years of obedience and hard work were rewarded when the Lord called to him, "Come into the ark, you and your household" (Genesis 7:1). The ark's one door opened to Noah's family and his zoo. Shortly afterward the rain began to fall.

Noah witnessed the flooding of the earth, riding out a storm of, well, biblical proportions. He was aware that the rest of humanity was lost in the churning waters. He and his family eventually faced the task of rebuilding and repopulating the earth.

Jesus connected His coming Kingdom to the flood and used the story of Noah to warn us of God's judgment and to give us a picture of His mercy and grace. The story points the way to salvation: through a door. Do you see the pattern and yet another example of "first the natural and afterward the spiritual"?

Since God "desires all men to be saved and to come to the knowledge of the truth" (1 Timothy 2:4), He established a pattern for salvation. Noah's family entered the ark through one door. Thousands of years later the pattern was repeated in the gospel of John when Jesus said, "I am the door" and "I am the way, the truth, and the life. No one comes to the Father except through Me" (John 10:9; 14:6).

Noah's name, in spite of the tumultuous life he lived, also foreshadowed what Jesus came to offer: "Come to Me, all you who labor and are heavy laden, and I will give you rest" (Matthew 11:28). The arrival of His Kingdom will finally bring rest to a weary world.

The New Ark of Israel

In 1897 in Basel, Switzerland, Theodor Herzl, known as the father of Zionism, began to build a new "ark" by organizing the first Zionist Congress. Herzl was not a religious man, but God used him to begin the fulfillment of prophecy: the rebirth of Israel after nearly two thousand years.

With approximately two hundred delegates from seventeen countries in agreement, Herzl defined their primary goal: "Zionism aims at establishing for the Jewish people a publically and assured home in Palestine."[3] The word *Zion* is the ancient spiritual name for Jerusalem: "Therefore thus says the Lord God: 'Behold, I lay in

Zion a stone for a foundation, a tried stone, a precious cornerstone, a sure foundation'" (Isaiah 28:16).

Herzl wrote in his diary, "In Basel I founded the Jewish State...maybe in five years, certainly in fifty, everyone will realize it."[4] The fulfillment of Ezekiel 36–37 had begun. Fifty years later, on November 29, 1947, the United Nations approved Resolution 181, which called for partitioning Palestine into two states: one for the Jewish people and one for Palestinians. The next year the independent state of Israel was born on May 14, 1948.

God is building an ark for His chosen people through the nation of Israel. He continues to call His people back to the Promised Land, but in this regathering they are not coming just from Babylon, as they did centuries ago. This time they are coming from all over the world.

Israel is an ark, offering a homeland for a weary people. As Noah's ark was a sign of judgment and salvation, so the rebirth of Israel is a sign to the world that the Lord's kingdom is coming soon.

"For the LORD shall build up Zion; He shall appear in His glory.... This will be written for the generation to come, that a people yet to be created may praise the LORD" (Psalm 102:16, 18). The phrase "generation to come" in Hebrew means the last generation. Who will be the last generation? Those who see Zion being built up, which we are witnessing today. You and I could be part of the last generation.

The End of the Age Begins

Many years ago a friend introduced me to Arnold Fruchtenbaum. A graduate of Dallas Theological Seminary, he has written a number of books that bring us a rich new understanding of the Jewish roots of Christianity. In *Footsteps of the Messiah*, Fruchtenbaum discusses the Olivet discourse and the signs of Jesus's return. Every Christian is eager to know the signs of Christ's coming. This was true as well of his first followers.

"What will be the sign of your coming and of the end of the age?" His disciples had asked Jesus. He answered with one specific sign: "Nation will rise against nation, and kingdom against kingdom. There will be famines and earthquakes in various places. All these are the beginning of birth pains" (Matthew 24:3, 7–8, NIV).

Earlier, Jesus spoke of wars between various nations, but this alone was not the sign of the end of the age. He defined exactly when the end would begin, saying, "Nation will rise against nation, and kingdom against kingdom." This has a specific meaning.

Fruchtenbaum writes: "This expression is a Hebrew idiom for a world war. What Jesus stated here is that when there is a world war, rather than merely a local war, that world war would signal that the end of the age had begun."[5]

That could make World War I (1914–1918) the beginning of the end of the age, the first of many "birth pains." During that war something miraculous happened in Jerusalem (in 1917). The British general Edmund Allenby marched with his army into Jerusalem on December 9, 1917, the eve of Hanukkah. The general dismounted and entered the city on foot out of respect for the holy city. After four hundred years of Turkish rule, the Turks fled Jerusalem, surrendering the city in a bloodless battle.

Liberating Jerusalem from the Turks was another step toward building the new ark of Israel. While Hanukkah is not one of the seven ordained feasts, it is the most historically documented Jewish holiday. Called the Feast of Lights, Hanukkah celebrates the rededication of the temple and independence from oppression in 165 BC.[6] Jesus celebrated Hanukkah as the Feast of Dedication (see John 10:22). The symbolism of General Allenby's victory on the eve of Hanukkah was not lost on the Jewish people.

Predictions and Patterns

Many prophecies in the Bible have multiple fulfillments. God establishes patterns to help us understand and learn from the past. The events and prophecies of the past also are prophecies for the future. For instance, Noah's ark looks ahead to Israel as the ark in the twentieth and twenty-first centuries. The near-sacrifice of Isaac foreshadows Jesus's death on a cross. In Israel's long history of scattering and regathering, each cycle brings us closer to the Messiah's appearance.

Like my history book with the overlaying transparencies, in which I turn pages to flesh out the past, we can lay down some transparencies of the future and try to get an idea of what is coming.

The Fifty-Years Pattern

Patterns give us a window to the future. One of the patterns revolves around the concept of fifty years and the Jewish year of Jubilee. "For six years you may plant your fields and prune your vineyards and harvest your crops, but during the seventh year the land will enjoy a Sabbath year of rest to the LORD," God told His people. "Count off seven Sabbath years, seven years times seven, adding up to forty-nine years in all. Then on the Day of Atonement of the fiftieth year, blow the trumpets loud and long throughout the land" (Leviticus 25:3–4, 8–9, NLT).

The fiftieth year became the Year of Jubilee, when all hired workers were set free and all bond slaves released. All land was restored to its original owner, and all debts were forgiven. This holy, life-giving year was ushered in with celebration.

Think back to Theodor Herzl and his 1897 proclamation of a Jewish state. Fifty years later, in 1947, the United Nations ratified Israel's statehood.

We talked about the miracle of General Allenby's liberation of Jerusalem in 1917. Exactly fifty years later, in 1967, the Six-Day War put East Jerusalem and the Temple Mount back into the hands of the Jewish people. Soldiers wept as they prayed freely for the first time at the Western Wall, the closest they could come to worshiping where the temple once stood.

What will we see fifty years into the future?

Revival

God promised Abraham, "In you all the families of the earth shall be blessed" (Genesis 12:3). This is an amazing promise that propels the blessings of Abraham far into the future. The prophecies and patterns of Abraham's life set into motion the plan to bless the world through the Abrahamic Covenant. Every time God visibly fulfills prophecy concerning the Jewish people and Israel, He pours out His Holy Spirit on the church, and the church is renewed and reawakened. Within seven years of the first Zionist Congress, God began to move in a powerful way, by His Holy Spirit, in and through the church.

When the Spirit falls, we see renewed hearts, changed and blessed lives. Reading a history of revivals gives one the sense of a great pattern designed to impact not just the church but the secular world as well.

The Welsh Revival

The 1904 revival that broke out in Wales changed that small nation. Evan Roberts was a young coal miner who prayed fervently for revival. He was given a vision: a check endorsed to him in the amount of one hundred thousand souls.

Roberts and a handful of people began meeting in a tiny church, praying together for the vision to be fulfilled. As they waited on the Lord, the Holy Spirit was poured out, and a great revival swept through Wales. Taverns and brothels were closed for lack of business. Meetings were held almost every evening for more than a year. More than 150,000 souls made commitments to follow Jesus. Relationships were healed. Drunkenness and theft diminished. People worked more diligently, paid their bills more regularly. The whole society was changed.[7]

Azusa Street

Two years later William J. Seymour, an African American preacher and the son of former slaves, became an answer to prayer. In 1906 a small and faithful group of women gathered to petition the Lord for revival in Los Angeles. While they prayed one day, Pastor Seymour—a man blind in one eye—knocked on their door. Wondering what this stranger wanted, they opened the door a crack. With quiet confidence, Seymour told them he had come in response to their prayers.

Seymour and a small band of followers began meeting in a home on Bonnie Brea Street. As he preached on the power and manifestation of the Holy Spirit, revival broke out and their numbers grew. They leased a rundown building at 312 Azusa Street. Originally built as an African Methodist Episcopal church in a poor section of town, it had since served as a wholesale house, a lumberyard, a tombstone shop, and a stable with rooms for rent upstairs. Seymour and his wife, Jennie, cleaned and prepared the building for services, installing benches of simple planks set on nail kegs. These were humble circumstances, but it didn't stop people from every level of society from coming to hear Seymour preach. They were experiencing the presence of God's Spirit.

God's glory would appear as a cloud or mist that would fill the room and glow. Meetings went on around the clock. Some people came with great faith and a desire to participate. Others came with skepticism—until they were unable to resist what they saw. The blind could see, the deaf could hear, and the lame could walk. For more than seven years, God manifested His glory through healings, salvation, and great miracles.

Spiritual Explosion

Two strong church movements grew out of that revival: the Pentecostal and charismatic churches that are credited with spearheading the fastest-growing segment of Christianity around the world. Remember, just a few years before these revivals broke out, the first Zionist Congress in 1897 initiated plans for the state of Israel. As God began gathering His people to the homeland He had promised to Abraham, so He also called His church back to Pentecost of the first-century, to salvation, to holiness, to the power of the Holy Spirit, and looking for the imminent return of Jesus.

The twentieth century progressed through two world wars, reinforcing the great sign of the end of the age: nation against nation. The prophet Isaiah's question, "Can a country be born in a day?" (66:8, NIV), was answered when Israel was recognized as a sovereign nation on May 14, 1948.

In the natural world we saw a new nation. The result? A spiritual explosion, as God raised up voices and ministries that began to impact the world. In 1949, the year after the rebirth of Israel, twenty-nine-year-old Billy Graham launched a crusade in Los Angeles that vaulted him into the public eye. He was known universally as a powerful evangelist who ultimately preached to more people in person than anyone else in history. Two years later, in 1951, another twenty-nine-year-old—Bill Bright—launched a worldwide ministry on the campus of UCLA, energizing thousands of young volunteers with a passion for evangelism and discipleship. Those are just two of many who answered God's call.

Right after the Six-Day War in 1967, the Jesus People revival of the late sixties and seventies captured many hearts—including mine—and gave birth to the modern messianic movement as thousands of Jews accepted Jesus as their Messiah.

We are living in a time of unprecedented growth for Christianity. According to statistics provided by the Center for the Study of Global Christianity, some 2.3 billion Christians were alive in 2010. The largest single block, some 588 million, is still found in Europe. Latin America, however, is already close behind with 544 million. Africa has more than 493 million. And Asia has 352 million. One estimate is that by 2025 there will be 2.6 billion believers in the world.[8]

The Muslim world, too, is experiencing a surge of faith as reports of Jesus revealing Himself through supernatural dreams and visions emerge. During the Islamic Revolution in Iran in 1979, there were barely five hundred known Christian believers in the country. By the 1980s there were a few thousand. Now, Christian workers in Iran believe there are a few million Iranian believers.[9] God's work in the lives of Muslims is fascinating. Remember, He made a promise to Ishmael when Abraham sent his first son into the desert. We are hearing reports of dreams and visions that reveal Jesus to Muslims in the Arab world and in nations such as Iran. For more information, I recommend Tom Doyle's book *Dreams and Visions* and his account of how Jesus is awakening the Muslim world.

I recently visited Iraq, where I met Muslims who shared their miraculous stories of coming to Christ and the high cost of following the beloved Savior they call Isa.

The outpouring of God's Spirit will continue to reach deeper and wider into populations of people who are hungry for the truth. "I will pour out My Spirit on all flesh; your sons and your daughters shall prophesy, your old men shall dream dreams, your young men shall see visions" (Joel 2:28), the Lord promised.

Peter repeated those words on Pentecost in the first century. But remember, the promise hinges on an era—the last days.

Daniel's Seventy Weeks

MOST OF OUR DISCUSSION OF PROPHESIED EVENTS
and signs of God's work in the last days has centered on revelations that God built
into what we think of as natural phenomena. He has revealed Himself, His character, His Son, the plan of salvation, and even details leading up to the first *and* the
second coming of the Messiah, Jesus. And all these can be read in signs from God
that involve no words.

We have looked at God's creation and His design of the heavens as well as the way
time is measured on the Jewish calendar, the significance of seasons and religious observances, and geopolitical developments, such as the rebirth of the nation of Israel. For
anyone who is attuned to these signs, the message is more than clear. But God did not
leave it at that. We know that He spoke through the prophets, giving them visions,
dreams, and words to tell the world of God, His nature, His work, and His plans for
the future. So let's look at one of the most celebrated of the Hebrew prophets: Daniel.

Daniel was uprooted and exiled to Babylon. But he and a few of the most promising Hebrew young men were selected for special training and education. He served
the government of Nebuchadnezzar, but he never forgot who he was—a son of
Judah, abducted from Jerusalem.

Daniel studied prophecy. He knew that the seventy years of desolation that
Jeremiah had prophesied (25:11) were coming to an end. He began to pray for the
rebuilding and restoration of the Holy City and the temple. As he prayed, he also

repented with fasting, sackcloth, and ashes on behalf of his people. The Lord responded through the angel Gabriel with a prophecy and a declaration that have kept
scholars, theologians, and prophecy buffs debating the most accurate interpretation
for more than two millenniums:

> Seventy weeks are determined
> For your people and for your holy city,
> To finish the transgression,
> To make an end of sins,
> To make reconciliation for iniquity,
> To bring in everlasting righteousness,
> To seal up vision and prophecy,
> And to anoint the Most Holy.
>
> Know therefore and understand,
> That from the going forth of the command
> To restore and build Jerusalem
> Until Messiah the Prince,
> There shall be seven weeks and sixty-two weeks;
> The street shall be built again, and the wall,
> Even in troublesome times. (Daniel 9:24–25)

Seventy weeks are commonly interpreted as four hundred ninety years (70 x 7 =
490), during which the Lord would accomplish six purposes for the Jewish people.
The first three of these purposes deal with the remedy for sin. The last three speak
of righteousness being established. The Lord established a pattern that would be
fulfilled only with the coming of the Messiah. Only a sacrifice that permanently
atones for sin can fulfill Daniel's prophecy. Jesus's dying on the cross did "make an
end of sins" and "reconciliation for iniquity."

The final three purposes will be fulfilled by the second coming of the Messiah,
for only He can establish "everlasting righteousness," fulfill all the prophecies, and

restore the true temple. Daniel was familiar with Jeremiah's writing and must have recognized Gabriel's message as a confirmation of Jeremiah's prophecy:

> "Behold, the days are coming," says the LORD,
> "That I will raise to David a Branch of righteousness;
> A King shall reign and prosper,
> And execute judgment and righteousness in the earth.
> In His days Judah will be saved,
> And Israel will dwell safely;
> Now this is His name by which He will be called:
>
> THE LORD OUR RIGHTEOUSNESS." (Jeremiah 23:5–6)

Daniel was given a precise mathematical prediction in Daniel 9:25. Before the Messiah or the Anointed One came, there would be a declaration to restore and rebuild Jerusalem, and 483 years (69 x 7 = 483) after that declaration, the Messiah would come.[1]

On March 14, 445 BC, Artaxerxes gave the command authorizing Nehemiah to restore and rebuild the walls and gates of the city of Jerusalem.[2] Exactly 483 years later Jesus entered the city of Jerusalem on a donkey, proclaiming Himself to be the Messiah. This occurred on the first Palm Sunday. By the end of that week, the Messiah was crucified, buried, and resurrected. The sixty-ninth week was fulfilled in just the way the angel had told Daniel it would be: "Messiah shall be cut off, but not for Himself" (Daniel 9:26). The crucifixion cut Jesus off for us; Jesus sacrificed Himself for us. But then Jesus rose from the dead on the third day.

Two Regatherings

Isaiah described two regatherings of Israel: "It shall come to pass in that day that the LORD shall set His hand again the second time to recover the remnant of His people who are left.… And gather together the dispersed of Judah from the four corners of the earth" (Isaiah 11:11–12).

The first regathering was in preparation for the first coming of the Messiah. The second regathering prepares for the second coming of the Messiah, when Jesus comes as King of kings and Lord of lords. The first regathering was from one place: Babylon. The second is from the four corners of the earth. There is no prophecy for a third regathering. There is no *third* coming of the Lord. Thus there is only one fulfillment of Daniel's seventieth week.

We are waiting for Daniel's final seven years to be fulfilled, known by many as the "seventieth week of Daniel." The seventieth week is seen as a set-apart time when God will judge the earth at the end of the church age. In terms of the calendar of the feasts of the Lord, this would be the end of the summer harvest. The seventieth week of Daniel also is known as the tribulation period, of which three and a half years are the great tribulation. This is the week all the judgments of God are poured out on the earth: the seal judgments, the trumpet judgments, and the seven bowls filled with the wrath of God (described in Revelation 6–11, 15–16). The pouring out of God's wrath will be utterly radical in every way: pestilence, terror, famine, natural disasters, wars, and demonic activity. I do not believe the church will experience this final seven years, "For God did not appoint us to wrath, but to obtain salvation through our Lord Jesus Christ" (1 Thessalonians 5:9).

Since prophecy is both prediction and pattern, and patterns come to light only when similar events repeat themselves, we must ask: What about the two regatherings spoken of in Isaiah?

When patterns converge, when the heavens send their signals, when the earth is in the early stages of "birth pains" (Matthew 24:8, NIV), it is time to "look up and lift up your heads, because your redemption draws near" (Luke 20:28).

Set Apart

God made promises to His people to set them apart during times of judgment. Let's look at Moses. He was sent to the Jewish people as a leader and to the court of Pharaoh as a prophet. In the name of the Lord, he said, "Let My people go."

When Pharaoh refused, God brought judgment in the form of plagues, which grew increasingly severe. During the first three plagues, all the people suffered, including the Jews. Before the fourth plague, however, God separated the children of Israel from the Egyptians. He set them apart in the land of Goshen, ensuring they would be safe from the plagues that would follow. They were untouched by the final seven plagues, so they would know that the Lord was in their midst (see Exodus 8:23).

Isaiah also prophesied the Lord's promise of protection from judgment: "Come, my people, enter your chambers, and shut your doors behind you; hide yourself, as it were, for a little moment, until the indignation is past" (26:20).

Being Ready

In my heart I can't help but return to my early Jesus People roots. I find myself singing Larry Norman's song again: "I wish we'd all been ready."[3] Larry has gone on to be with the Lord, but I'll always be grateful for the sense of urgency his music instilled in me. There is no question Jesus wants us to be ready. He told His disciples about His return:

> It is like a man going to a far country, who left his house and gave authority
> to his servants, and to each his work, and commanded the doorkeeper to
> watch. Watch therefore, for you do not know when the master of the house
> is coming—in the evening, at midnight, at the crowing of the rooster, or in
> the morning—lest, coming suddenly, he find you sleeping. And what I say
> to you, I say to all: Watch! (Mark 13:34–37)

Jesus also told them the parable of the ten virgins waiting for the bridegroom. Each had her own lamp and was supposed to save enough oil to keep her lamp burning. As Jesus taught the lesson, five were ready for the bridegroom, but five were not.

And the foolish said to the wise, "Give us some of your oil, for our lamps are going out." But the wise answered, saying, "No, lest there should not be enough for us and you; but go rather to those who sell, and buy for yourselves." And while they went to buy, the bridegroom came, and those who were ready went in with him to the wedding; and the door was shut.

Afterward the other virgins came also, saying, "Lord, Lord, open to us!" But he answered and said, "Assuredly, I say to you, I do not know you." (Matthew 25:8–12)

The oil that was searched for by the five foolish virgins is a symbol of the Holy Spirit and of salvation. This is a strong warning. Some have not trusted sincerely in Jesus Christ. We need to keep our lamps burning and keep enough oil in reserve so we can watch through the night.

Is Jesus your Lord and Savior? Is He the Bridegroom you are watching for? Is your life filled with the Holy Spirit? "Watch therefore, for you know neither the day nor the hour in which the Son of Man is coming" (Matthew 25:13).

That Which Was Spoken

You may be asking yourself, What am I supposed to do with all this? Remember, "Prophecy is the mold into which history is poured."[4] Jesus often told His disciples what was going to happen, and usually they didn't understand. But after His words came to pass, they were able to say, "This is what was spoken by…," just as Peter did during Pentecost, when Joel's prophecy was fulfilled (Acts 2:16–21).

This is one reason it is important for us to be students of the Word, so we can know His promises and recognize them when they are fulfilled. Our Father has told us the future in order to give us a quiet confidence and great strength. The kingdom of God was the heart of the Messiah's message. "But seek the kingdom of God, and all these things shall be added to you," He taught. "Do not fear, little flock, for it is your Father's good pleasure to give you the kingdom" (Luke 12:31–32).

Matthew 24:14 tells us, "And this gospel of the kingdom will be preached in all the world as a witness to all the nations, and then the end will come." This is the message the Lord wants the whole world to hear before He returns. It was the message of John the Baptist, who preached, "Repent, for the kingdom of heaven is at hand" (Matthew 3:2). It was Jesus's message: "Repent, for the kingdom of heaven is at hand" (Matthew 4:17). This same message is ours today, and it is also our prayer: "Your kingdom come. Your will be done.... For Yours is the kingdom and the power and the glory forever. Amen" (Matthew 6:10, 13).

The Jewish people held a deep longing and expectation for the kingdom that would be ushered in by the Messiah. Too many of them missed the need and importance of the Messiah as Savior. Many believers today focus narrowly on Jesus as Savior and miss His role as coming King.[5]

Step Without Fear

Each of us must make a choice every day to step into the story of what God is doing in the world. We do this with the confidence that Jesus is with us every step of the way. When I first began to contemplate the Season of Destiny, the Lord gave me a specific word for my congregation. In light of everything going on—locally, globally, geopolitically, financially, emotionally—as well as the many personal circumstances that threaten to overwhelm us, the word from the Lord is this: *Do not be afraid.* Over and over, God tells us not to be afraid.

The Bible has 365 verses that whisper, shout, admonish, exhort, comfort, and encourage us: *Do not be afraid. Fear not. God has not given us the spirit fear. Do not let your hearts be troubled and do not be afraid. Be anxious for nothing.* There's a promise for every day of the year. Your life is precious to the Lord. He sees the big picture: the prophetic story of the entire universe unfolding rapidly around us. But He also sees and numbers the hairs on your head (see Matthew 10:30). He gives us signs and signals because He loves us.

During this season, remember God's Word to the prophet Amos: "Surely the

Lord GOD does nothing, unless He reveals His secret to His servants the prophets" (3:7). We are His servants and His beloved children. Listen for His Word, watch for His signals, and pray for our King's soon return. Maranatha!

As I close this chapter on patterns and prophecy, I am thinking of that book of photographs and overlays that enabled me to look at the Roman Colosseum in its various stages. I can add another layer to the story because I recently learned how this massive, extraordinary structure was built in an unprecedented ten years or less. (Most of Rome's beautiful ancient structures were built over decades if not hundreds of years.)

After the destruction of Jerusalem and the second temple in AD 70, Emperor Titus forced thousands of Jews from Jerusalem into slavery. He brought them to Rome to build an arena where more than half a million people and a million animals would die violently. That is how the famous structure was built in no more than a decade.

Then I learned how the mighty Colosseum eventually deteriorated to the ruins we see today. Earthquakes and other forces weakened the structure, but ultimately much of its marble, limestone, and travertine were carried away to build churches, including the Vatican.

Again we see a natural example of a spiritual principle. Churches were built using ancient stones quarried and hauled and lifted in backbreaking labor by thousands of Jewish slaves. It is a picture of reality. Once again the Jewish people became the pillars of our faith.[6]

I was soon to say good-bye to one of those pillars.

How NASA Research Clarifies Biblical Prophecy

THE HEAVENS ONCE WERE A MAGICAL CANOPY OF FIERY daylight, cooled at night by the glow of the moon. Twinkling lights spread their star stories across the universe.

When I was young, imagining myself as an astronomer or astronaut, I was endlessly intrigued by the mystery of God's lights and learned everything I could. They spoke to me in the rhythms of creation, and I felt God's presence, especially after the night I first met Him at the age of eleven. I'd lie in the yard outside my home and listen to crickets and the wind in the trees. I would stare at the sky, marveling at the faraway lights signaling God's glory. I eventually learned the fanciful legends of Orion, Cassiopeia, and the menagerie of lions, bulls, dogs, and rams. Then I grew up.

The science of astronomy had a way of removing the awe and glory from God's work in the sky. The moon, sun, and stars were said to be gaseous balls of fire or dark, icy matter. They were the beautiful part of creation that ordered the days and nights and the seasons. But I no longer heard the stories, and for me the heavenly bodies lost their mystery.

That is, until Mark Biltz, a Bible teacher who looks for confirmations of God's work and His Word, came along. In addition to studying the Hebrew origins of the Christian faith, Biltz searches creation for confirmations of God's truth. He convinced me that the stories God wants us to know are still found in the heavens.

He has studied NASA's records of lunar and solar eclipses alongside a chart of the seven Jewish feasts that are ordained in the book of Leviticus. I knew of the feasts, especially Passover and how it foreshadowed the coming of Jesus the Messiah. But this teacher not only demonstrated how all seven feasts point to Jesus; he also tied them to celestial events. The world God created confirms His work with humanity. God does not want us to miss out on His Kingdom and His plans for the end of this age. He has tried to make sure we get the message by providing that message in a number of places and in a variety of ways.

Blood Moons

Biltz was raised in a devout Catholic home where all the kids went to seminary and convent schools. But his family on his father's side was Jewish, so they celebrated a Passover Seder every year.

"A branch without roots is dead!" he exclaims. "Christianity thinks it's a new tree, but we are not! We are the branch that got grafted in. If we don't acknowledge that truth, we miss out on the richness that God poured into the alpha tree, the Hebrew people."

One day he saw a dramatic photograph of a large red moon, indicating a total eclipse, directly over the Dome of the Rock in Jerusalem. The blood-red moon looked like a signal, a sign. Biltz began a quest.

While searching NASA's website, he discovered that all the eclipses from thousands of years past to thousands of years into the future are recorded. A total eclipse, as opposed to a partial one, causes the moon to appear blood red. The very rare occurrence of four blood moons in succession is called a tetrad.[1]

Then he examined the Hebrew calendar in conjunction with NASA's list of total lunar eclipses. NASA projects that we will experience a tetrad in 2014 and 2015. And the four lunar eclipses will fall on the first day of the biblical feasts of Passover and

Tabernacles, two years in a row. Biltz wondered if this had ever happened before. Is there a pattern in this? If there is, did anything prophetic happen during the past tetrads?

By charting previous total lunar eclipses that fell on Jewish feast days, he found sets of four lunar eclipses in the last century, most recently in 1967 and 1968. Two months before the Six-Day War, a blood moon appeared on the first day of Passover, April 24, 1967. Another blood moon appeared later that year, on October 18, the Feast of Tabernacles. The pattern was repeated in 1968, completing the tetrad. The 1967 war gained Israel the Sinai Peninsula, the Golan Heights, the Gaza Strip, the West Bank, and most important, East Jerusalem, including the Temple Mount.

In 1949–1950, right after Israel became a nation, blood moons appeared on the first day of Passover and Tabernacles, again two years in a row. Going further back, Biltz found no incidences of blood moon tetrads falling on feast days in the 1800s, 1700s, or 1600s. But in 1492, after the Jews were expelled from Spain during the Spanish Inquisition, four blood moons occurred in 1493 and 1494 on the feasts of Passover and Tabernacles.

A pattern emerged! Every time there have been four blood moons on the first days of the feasts of Passover and Tabernacles two years in a row, something significant has occurred involving the Jewish people.

Eclipses and Their Meanings

A passage in the Talmud says, "When the sun is in eclipse, it is a bad omen for the whole world.... When the moon is in eclipse, it is a bad omen for Israel, since Israel reckons by the moon and idolaters by the sun."[2] And the prophet Joel wrote, "The sun shall be turned into darkness, and the moon into blood, before the coming of the great and awesome day of the LORD" (Joel 2:31).

So Biltz began to wonder about the prophetic significance of solar eclipses. The Lord also said through Joel that the sun would turn dark (see 2:10). Biltz went back to the NASA website and correlated solar eclipses to the biblical calendar. On the biblical date Nisan 1, God instructed Moses to change the calendar. The calendar originally began in the fall, but God told Moses to begin the religious calendar in the spring. Significantly, on Nisan 1, Moses set up the tabernacle (see Exodus 40).

After noting the shift in the Hebrew calendar, Biltz was astonished when he learned what is projected by NASA for 2014–2015: a total lunar eclipse on the first day of Passover and the first day of Tabernacles in 2014 and a total eclipse of the sun in 2015 on Nisan 1, the first day of the religious calendar. Two weeks later on Passover, a total lunar eclipse will occur, then a partial solar eclipse on the Feast of Trumpets, followed by a total eclipse of the moon on the Feast of Tabernacles in 2015. After 2015, there are no more tetrads of blood moons on the Jewish feast days for the rest of this century.

The years 2014 and 2015 could be extremely significant prophetically. God speaks to us in the natural, giving pictures and clues of His spiritual promises and plans. Remember the rule of interpretation: first the natural and then the spiritual. God establishes patterns that are repeated, and His meanings become increasingly clear with each overlay.

Will something happen in the Middle East in 2014–2015? I don't know. Only God knows. As I write this, the civil war in Syria has dragged on past the two-and-a-half-year mark. Hezbollah, a Shi'ah Muslim faction based in Lebanon on Israel's northern border, has joined the conflict in support of the Assad regime. And on Israel's southern border, the elected president of Egypt has been removed from office by the country's military leaders. Once again, Egypt in the post–Hosni Mubarak era has unpredictable national leaders and an uncertain political future.

On the one hand, we know the Middle East is a tinderbox. It has been an ongoing tale of unrest and instability dating back to Abraham's banishment of Ishmael. But in another sense, the greatest unrest today—and it is spreading—affects Muslim nations. Afghanistan prepares for a resurgence of Taliban extortion and menace, and Allied troops continue to demobilize, turning over responsibility for internal security to the Afghan government. While Afghanistan is not a Middle Eastern nation, it has been the scene of much radical Islamic activity along with neighboring Pakistan, which possesses nuclear weapons.

It is not difficult to picture the growing instability in Muslim nations escalating into regional conflicts and an international war. Already, armed conflict that had been contained within the borders of one nation has reached across borders into neighboring countries. What will be the prophetic significance of geopolitical and military developments in the Middle East at the time of the next tetrads in 2014 and 2015? I can't say or even offer an educated guess. My pastor, Chuck Smith, is known around the world as a prophecy teacher. Remember, he once said, "Prophecy is best understood after it has come to pass."

Mark Biltz has studied blood moons and solar eclipses in conjunction with the Jewish feasts. I asked him what he believes might come to pass with the next tetrad. In response he said he can only present this material and let others give it serious consideration.

I have regained my earlier wonder and sense of awe at all that God has put in the heavens. It is there for our enjoyment, to be sure. It also is there to declare God's glory. But there is a third reason: it is there to remind us and to reveal to us that God is at work. He is working out His plans for the end of the age. God tells us stories through the stars.

> The heavens declare the glory of God;
> And the firmament shows His handiwork.
> Day unto day utters speech,
> And night unto night reveals knowledge.
> There is no speech nor language
> Where their voice is not heard.
> Their line has gone out through all the earth,
> And their words to the end of the world. (Psalm 19:1–4)

Did the Jews Discover America?

Just as we see signs of God's future work in the heavens, we also get clues to the origins of past events in history—including the discovery of America. As the darkness of the Inquisition swept through Spain and parts of Europe in the late fifteenth century, an explorer and navigator prepared to embark on an expedition that would change the map of the world. Recorded in personal diaries, some of the details of his voyage later appeared in a volume titled *The Book of Prophecies,* published around 1501. The book is a collection of the author's writings, spiritual insights, favorite Scriptures, literary passages, and prophetic statements. In the diaries, Christopher Columbus expressed an unabashed passion for Israel.

Tisha B'Av (the Jewish day of mourning) has shaped not only Jewish history. In 1492 the ominous events surrounding the ninth of Av forced a commissioned explorer to set off on a journey months before he had intended—with history-changing ramifications. This is all noted in the historical record, yet in school we were not taught that these factors contributed to Columbus's expedition.

I was astounded when I discovered *The Book of Prophecies.* Columbus wrote the book in the late fifteenth century as he watched the tribunal of the holy office of the Inquisition, which was established to maintain religious orthodoxy, regularly terrorize the accused. People were exiled or burned at the stake. The inquisitors targeted Jews, who had multiplied over the centuries in Europe. Jewish *conversos* (converts) were arrested, accused, and condemned by secret evidence and unnamed informers. The converts were tortured until they confessed to being heretics, and then they were executed.[3]

The immigration of Jews into Europe had escalated after the destruction of the temple in AD 70. Even before the time of Jesus, Jews had begun settling in the Iberian Peninsula. They were called Sephardim, from the Hebrew term for Spain, *Sepharad* (see Obadiah 1:20). The growth and reputation of this Jewish community drew the apostle Paul to visit Spain (see Romans 15:24–28).

In the 1400s the Sephardim community included Columbus. His faith has long been established, confirmed by much of his own writing. His possible Jewish ancestry has also been examined and hotly debated. Was Columbus Jewish? The evidence is compelling. "The story of Jews in America begins with Christopher Columbus," declares one anti-Semitic source, *The International Jew: The World's Foremost Problem,* written by none other than Henry Ford, the industrialist and automobile manufacturer.[4] His book appears on a Muslim website.

Several Jewish resources, including the Jewish American Hall of Fame, claim the explorer as one of their own: "It was Spanish Jewry, not Spanish jewelry, that paid for Columbus' voyage of discovery," they insist. "There is no question that it was his Spanish-Jewish friends who were instrumental in arranging for his meeting with the Spanish monarchs in 1486 and who turned his dream into reality."[5]

Columbus's vision and scientific knowledge earned the Spanish king and queen's favor. And he raised the needed funds from Jewish conversos. (Louis de Santangel, chancellor of the royal household, and Gabriel Sanchez, treasurer of Aragon, were conversos.) With the finances arranged, he embarked on his voyage.

But it was a dangerous time for all Jews, even favored ones. A royal edict demanded the expulsion of all Jews from Spain by August 2, 1492. This coincided with Tisha B'Av, the Jewish day of mourning. So Columbus gathered his crew, boarded the three ships, and set sail for the New World on the morning of August 3, 1492. With this action he obeyed the edict of expulsion along with almost three hundred thousand other Jews.

Here are some more intriguing facts:

- There is evidence that Columbus spoke Spanish while living in Italy, an unusual situation unless his family had originated in Spain. Spanish-speaking Jewish refugees from the Inquisition were numerous in the Italian area of Genoa.
- The form Colón, which Columbus adopted as the Spanish equivalent of his last name, is not the expected form (which would have been Colom or Colombo). It was, however, a common Jewish variation of the name.
- Columbus was known to frequent the company of Jews and former Jews, among whom were notable astronomers and navigators as well as his official translator. *Marranos* (another term for Jews forced to convert to Catholicism) figured prominently among Columbus's backers and crew. Throughout his life he demonstrated a keen knowledge of the Bible and the geography of the Holy Land.
- Columbus began his diary of his first voyage to America: "In the same month in which their Majesties [Ferdinand and Isabella] issued the

edict that all Jews should be driven out of the kingdom and its territories, in the same month they gave me the order to undertake with sufficient men my expedition."[6] The order of expulsion was signed March 31, 1492. Columbus was apparently privy to the information about the expulsion of the Jews and made his plans accordingly.

- The fact that the expulsion of Spanish Jewry and Columbus's voyage coincided is telling. Even when Columbus was scheduled to set sail on August 3, he insisted that his crew be aboard his vessels a day earlier. Hundreds of thousands of Jews were deported from Spain on August 2, 1492.

- This coincidence of dates was first noted by Spanish biographer S. de Madariaga. The English Jewish historian Cecil Roth also commented on the "coincidence" of August 2, 1492, being on Tisha B'Av, the Jewish fast of mourning. It was as if Columbus had arranged to remain on board ship for that ominous day and to depart afterward.[7]

Chosen for a Mission

As I read *The Book of Prophecies,* I began to see the discovery of America and current politics in a new light. Columbus truly believed he was on a mission from God. Over and over in his logs he dedicated his voyage to the Lord Jesus Christ. He brilliantly combined and used the practical knowledge gathered by scientists of his time, but in the letter he drafted to King Ferdinand and Queen Isabella to make his appeal, he said, "I base what I say only on holy and sacred scripture."[8]

Columbus possessed a sense of destiny that he was chosen for a mission, confirmed by his name, Christ-Topher ("Christ-bearer"). He was motivated by prophecy as much as a hunger for global discovery. In his *Book of Prophecies,* he collected passages from the Bible that inspired him to plan his voyage. These include Proverbs 8:27, which speaks of the earth's surface as being curved; Isaiah 40:22, the spherical earth; and the ocean currents mentioned in Isaiah 43:16. He later described his discovery of the New World as "the fulfillment of what Isaiah prophesied" in describing "isles beyond the sea" in Isaiah 24:15 and 60:9.[9]

He also suspected the existence of the American continent. He appears to have owned the 1472 edition of *Bibliothecae Historicae,* written by Diodorus Siculus, a first-century BC Greek historian who spoke of "a very great island many days sailing from Africa." Even beyond the geographical evidence Columbus collected, *The Book of Prophecies* shows an uncanny knowledge of prophetic events, a vision for the future, foresight, a deep faith—and a mission. Columbus wanted nothing less than the universal conversion to Christ of all people.[10]

The book was compiled with the help of an anonymous Italian scribe to whom Columbus indicated which passages he wanted copied, including several passages from an anthology of the works of Augustine published in Venice in 1491. Columbus also quoted the book of Isaiah and a lengthy commentary by a fourteenth-century Franciscan monk on the prophetic eighth chapter of Daniel. He chose passages from various sources that seemed to lend support to his personal role in fulfilling the prophecy.

Here are a few passages from *The Book of Prophecies* that I find spiritually and historically fascinating:

- "In the final year you will come to the land that has been returned by means of the sword and has been created by many peoples upon the mountains of Israel" (referencing the words of Ezekiel 38).[11]
- "The sons of Ishmael...will be the leaders of the persecution of Christians in the final days of the world."[12]
- In the introduction to *The Book of Prophecies,* editor Roberto Rusconi writes: "Columbus began to view the goal of the liberation of Jerusalem from Moslem domination in a more apocalyptic sense...the discovery of the West Indies became identified in his mind with one of the events which would precede the end of the world...and the universal conversion of the peoples to the gospel of Christ."[13]

- Think about this quote from Augustine: "With these and similar prophecies it is shown that what we know to have been fulfilled by Christ has been predicted: the God of Israel, who we know to be the one true God, will be worshipped not only by the one nation that is called Israel, but by all people, and that He will throw out the false gods of the Gentiles from their temples and from the hearts of their worshippers."[14] When this passage was written and later quoted, there was no physical nation of Israel—and there hadn't been since AD 70.

The book includes numerous prophetic references to Muslim domination and the conflict between Muslims, Christians, and Jews. Columbus held the same passion and regard for Jerusalem and God's people as many Christians do today.

Columbus remains a controversial figure. He has been variously described as one of the greatest mariners in history, a visionary genius, a mystic, a man of faith, a hero, a failed administrator, and a naive entrepreneur. He has also been described as a ruthless and greedy imperialist and the man most responsible for the near-genocide of America's native population.

But was he Jewish? The evidence points heavily in that direction. We know he had a unique call in life, and he fulfilled that call. Columbus's mission, begun in the crucible of persecution, was fueled by his passion to evangelize the world in anticipation of the second coming of Jesus.

But what of the future? Does America have a place in prophecy? This is a central question for Christians in the West as we wrestle with the meaning and interpretation of biblical prophecy.

The prophecies Columbus envisioned are coming to pass in our time. Jews around the world are "coming home" to Israel. There is a great ingathering of God's chosen people from the four corners of the world as Jews return to the tiny Middle Eastern nation of Israel.

But are America and the mostly Gentile Christians of America part of the story?

PART 5

IT IS TIME TO STEP INTO THE PROPHETIC STORY

God Is Bringing His People Home

THE STUDY OF PROPHECY YIELDS MANY PRACTICAL spiritual benefits. It confirms our belief that God is sovereign and that He has a definite plan for the world. It encourages our faith when we see signs in the world that God is moving forward as things fall into place signaling the end of this age and the beginning of Christ's reign on earth. Other people read prophecy because it conveys a glimpse of the future that is not revealed in other religious traditions. But prophecy serves a much more important purpose.

The greater purpose revealed in prophecy is that God's people—both Jewish and Christian—join together to be part of what He is doing at this time in history. We have met Israeli Jews and Israeli Arabs, both Christian and Jewish—who have devoted their lives to their people, their nation, and the call of God on their lives.

But what about us, American Christians living on the other side of the world? It is not enough just to read a book or study prophecy the way we might study American literature or the history of ancient Egypt. This is God's work we learn about in the Bible from the mouths of the ancient prophets. And it is His work we see unfolding today in the Middle East. As the prophesied events continue to unfold, the entire world will be affected. I do not exaggerate when I teach this truth: Israel is the center of our world, indeed of our history and our future. To understand God, His work on earth, history, and the future—including God's plans for the end of the age—we must understand and stand in support of Israel. It is our opportunity now to get involved in advance of the warfare that will precede God's judgment.

God's Advance Men in Israel

Juan and Jose don't sound like Jewish names, but they were Israeli citizens when I met them, telling me their stories of *aliyah*—the last great Exodus of Jews on earth. This time, however, the movement of the people is back home to repopulate Israel.

Juan, who is a banker, and his wife have three children. Jose, who is a schoolteacher, and his wife have four. Both families led prosperous lives in Santiago, Argentina. But due to their Jewish heritage, their families could not live securely in that South American nation. Anti-Semitism, always an ominous undercurrent, had become overt and dangerous there. So Juan and Jose took their families to Israel where they would be free to be Jewish. With little money and few resources, they landed in a completely foreign, alien country.

"We knew no language," said Juan, speaking through a Spanish translator. "Not a word of Hebrew. We are learning everything new." But driven by a shared desire to come home, they were ready to "make aliyah." (Aliyah is a joyful, fearful, courageous, practical, and mystical act. The origin of the word means "ascent" in Hebrew, but the meaning of *aliyah* is "the act of Jews immigrating, coming home to Israel.")

In the Old Testament, returning to Israel after exile, banishment, or dispersion is defined as "going up" or "ascending." The exiles "went up" as they returned from captivity in Babylon (see Ezra 2:1, 59; Nehemiah 5–6). Cyrus, king of Persia, in 538 BC said to the children of Israel, "Who is among you of all His people? May his God be with him, and let him go up to Jerusalem which is in Judah" (Ezra 1:3; see also 2 Chronicles 36:23). Today, aliyah beckons the children of Israel from around the world. And Israel welcomes them with a warm embrace.

Everything Changed in 1948

The year 1948 shattered the darkness of the Diaspora with the rebirth of the Hebrew nation. And Jews who had been driven to the four corners of the earth were being drawn home.

Immigration had begun in earnest in the late 1880s, especially from Russia and Europe. But when the state of Israel was legally established, aliyah became a vital part of the process for building the new nation. Jews started pouring in from all over the world: Argentina, Bulgaria, Ethiopia, France, Germany, Iraq, Lithuania, Poland, Romania, Russia, Turkey, Yemen.

> The state of Israel will be open for Jewish immigration and the Ingathering
> of Exiles; it will foster the development of the country for the benefit of all
> inhabitants; it will be based on freedom, justice and peace as envisaged by
> the prophets of Israel.[1]

In 1950 the Israeli legislature enacted the Law of Return, which grants every Jew the right to immigrate and immediately become a citizen. Most nations make immigration a challenge. Israel not only encourages immigration but created the Jewish Absorption Agency (JAA) to help make aliyah reality.

Maya Neiger works for the JAA in Jerusalem, which offers education, lessons in Hebrew, housing, jobs, and help with navigating a foreign culture. Maya became a valuable contact and friend to me and others from my church as we decided to raise funds to help Jewish immigrants. "I am a fifth-generation Jew on my father's side," she told us. "My mother is a Holocaust survivor. She came to Israel on the day it was established in 1948. For me, this helps close the circle. Working for the agency is not a job; it is a mission, a way of life."

The largest numbers of immigrants come from "countries of distress," such as Argentina, where Jews are unwelcome, harassed, and actively persecuted. Argentina claims the largest Jewish community in the region because of an open immigration policy. But Argentina also welcomed Nazi war criminals after World War II. The atmosphere ranges from peaceful coexistence to intense anti-Semitism.

Like Jose and Juan, many Jews left behind their livelihoods and homes to escape persecution. Most lack adequate resources, often because their assets have been frozen by the Argentinean government. They do not have the finances available to make aliyah possible.

Israel Is People

Jews and Christians from around the world are stepping up to meet the need, supplying the finances needed to make aliyah possible for more and more people. Israel is not a history lesson or the key to a prophetic clock. It is people! People pour in from all over the world, hundreds of thousands of immigrants from hostile and friendly countries alike, people who are driven by idealism and a passion for a Jewish national identity. Some two hundred thousand have immigrated from the United States, and beyond the Holocaust survivors who came after World War II, more than double that number have made aliyah from Western Europe.[2]

No matter the reason, they continue to come. I understand Isaiah 49:22 to be an open invitation from the Lord to those who believe in the Messiah Jesus to enter the story:

> Behold, I will lift My hand in an oath to the nations,
> And set up My standard for the peoples;
> They shall bring your sons in their arms,
> And your daughters shall be carried on their shoulders.

As the spiritual descendants of Abraham, our father of faith (see Romans 4:1–3), we are responsible for accepting the Lord's invitation. We have seen this principle prove true in many contexts: what God does in the natural realm is a picture of what He is doing in the spiritual realm. Aliyah is part of a larger picture, a pattern God established ages ago.

Partnering with the Jews in Israel—the people who are described in the prophets' dreams and visions from thousands of years ago—is fulfilling, to be sure. But becoming close friends with them and then losing them is as hard to bear as any other intimate human relationship.

Bridging the Unbridgeable

My friend Ron Nachman died in early 2013, and I still grieve the loss. We had moved from being political acquaintances to close, personal friends. I will miss him, but I find great comfort in knowing we had done the impossible. He and I, together, had bridged the unbridgeable gulf.

I felt that gulf keenly about a year before Ron left us. I was standing on the long, bleak stretch of train tracks that leads into the mouth of what had been one of the most evil places in the world: Auschwitz, a Nazi death camp in Poland. The day was biting cold and hazy, adding to the sinister feel. The horror of such a place is compounded by knowing that the atrocities were often justified by Christians who perverted and twisted Christian theology. I felt the weight of being a Gentile as I peered across that wide chasm.

"Anti-Semites have hated Jews because Jews are Jewish—essentially for the Jewish belief in their chosenness, in their own national identity, and in the universal reach of their one God and his moral law," wrote George Gilder.[3]

Auschwitz and the other death camps of World War II epitomized that sentiment at its most horrifying, irrational level. Jews were murdered in gas chambers simply because the blood of Abraham, Isaac, and Jacob flowed through their veins.

What are Christians to do now, in light of the biblical admonition to bless Israel and in view of history, which documents thousands of years of violence against the Jews? Israel is far more than a good cause. For me, Israel became people I know and love—Jews and Gentiles. The people, as Botrus Mansour said, "who are here, with their feet on the ground." Ten years ago I asked God to let me know His chosen people and to bring me the people who could make that happen, and He delivered.

I was not the only Christian pastor that Ron Nachman befriended. But a genuine friendship developed between us. I felt our bond when Robert Mawire and I knelt in Ron's living room and prayed for Ron's healing. I was deeply moved when he stood in front of our congregation and, straight from his heart, thanked everyone.

As I finish this book I am planning a tour of Israel. As always, I'm excited. But someone will be missing. An energy and a spirit will not be there. I can picture the scene Dorit Nachman related to us of Ron running across the hills of Samaria, bounding from rock to rock, sharing his vision for the future city of Ariel while Dorit and others tried to keep up with him.

It's as if God reached down and found a servant He could use, like the Bible characters of old. I pray for Ron's family, especially his dear wife, and for the people of Ariel, who have never known another mayor. They must feel a bit like orphans.

I am thankful that though the gulf between Gentile and Jew still exists, it is being crossed, and in some cases, like with Ron and me, a bridge has been built. I pray that he found peace in the bosom of Abraham and that he knows his Messiah in all His glory.

My journey to understanding Israel is far from over. I learned recently that rabbinical traditions teach there are seventy layers of meaning to the sacred Scriptures—"seventy faces of Torah"—and that we only dabble in the first few.[4]

Just thinking about that is exciting! I am eager to go deeper.

Rebuilding the Heart of the Holy Land

THERE ARE UNDENIABLE SCRIPTURAL, HISTORICAL, practical, and spiritual reasons for taking an active role in what God is doing in Israel. My pastor, Chuck Smith, used to say, "Watch to see where God is working and join Him." God is working all over the world in wonderful ways, but especially in Israel.

Step into the Story

We are exhorted to be actively involved in the story of Israel. Even in ancient times, Gentiles were part of the redemption of Israel. In the sixth century BC, the Babylonians, under Nebuchadnezzar, conquered Judah and took most of the Jews captive for seventy years. When the Persian (or Achaemenid) Empire conquered Babylon, Cyrus II issued a decree allowing the Jews to return to Jerusalem to rebuild the city and the temple. A Gentile king accomplished what the Jews were not able to do for themselves: he opened a way for them to return home.

Much earlier, as Moses was demanding that Pharaoh release the Hebrew slaves, Egyptians furnished the fleeing Israelites with material goods, which helped them as they traveled to the Promised Land. We could come up with example after example: the faithfulness of Ruth, a native of Moab and the ancestor of King David and Jesus.

The family of Corrie ten Boom, Christians living in Holland who suffered greatly for hiding Jews in their home during the Nazi occupation. Oskar Schindler, a German factory owner who bent the rules to employ and thus shelter Jews during Hitler's unchecked attacked on European Jews. Today, a growing number of Christians actively support Israel and help Jews return to their homeland. It is clear that Gentiles are an integral part of God's plan to protect and assist His chosen people, and at no time in history has this been more important.

"He who scattered Israel will gather him," the prophet said (Jeremiah 31:10). God has called the Gentiles to help with the ingathering. "This is what the Sovereign LORD says: 'See, I will beckon to the Gentiles, I will lift up my banner to the peoples; they will bring your sons in their arms and carry your daughters on their shoulders'" (Isaiah 49:22, NIV).

One of the opportunities for American Christians to join in the ingathering of Jews to Israel is the Nehemiah Project. Just as Nehemiah of the Old Testament led a remnant of Jews back to Israel to restore the ancient walls of Jerusalem, I believe God has called us to share in the rebuilding of Israel. "Yes, I have loved you with an everlasting love; therefore with lovingkindness I have drawn you. Again I will build you, and you shall be rebuilt" (Jeremiah 31:3–4). Christians can be active participants in the fulfillment of Jeremiah's prophecy.

My desire is to help restore Jerusalem by rebuilding our relationship with God's people, offering tangible assistance and friendship. The Nehemiah Project is committed to sharing the love of Yeshua of Nazareth with His brothers and sisters who live in Israel.

American Friends of Ariel

I will always think of Ariel as Ron Nachman's beloved city. I am thankful that my church, through the Nehemiah Project, supports the American Friends of Ariel. Our church helped build Ariel's state-of-the-art radio communications center, the National Youth Leadership Development Park, and numerous other projects.[1]

Jewish Agency for Israel

The Jewish Agency for Israel (JAFI) facilitates the immigration of Jews to their spiritual homeland. In Hebrew, this is known as aliyah (discussed in chapter 21). JAFI has set up absorption centers designed to provide a soft landing for people immigrating to Israel. Absorption centers offer provisions and an immediate place to live, plus an opportunity to learn the Hebrew language and culture, develop job skills, make friends, find education, and adjust to a new homeland.

Our congregation gives to a fund that helps finance aliyah. When we conduct a tour of Israel, we include a stop at the Jewish Agency's absorption center, where we present a financial gift.

Far-Reaching Friends

Our church's relationship with Israel continued to deepen when we launched a student exchange program with the city of Ariel. Israeli high school students came to stay with San Diego families for a week, going to the beach and parks, touring Disneyland and the San Diego Zoo and Universal Studios, and hanging out with our high school teens. The Israeli students were accompanied by chaperones.

Long talks among the teenagers dissipated many false conceptions and misunderstandings. One girl, Sasha, sitting under the stars in a hot tub, told Elisabeth, a teenager from my church, that she was surprised at how much American students know about Israel and even the Holocaust.

"We study about them in church and school," Elisabeth explained.

"Why?"

"Because we love Israel and its history."

Sasha contemplated that for a moment and then said, "Most people don't like us, you know. This is very unusual."

By the week's end she knew that our love for her and her people was genuine.

Their visit to San Diego was followed by two weeks at a ranch in Northern California. The ranch's owners, Bruce Johnston and his wife, Heather, designed a program with an emphasis on Old Testament scriptures and songs. The Israeli teenagers also participated in ropes courses, river rafting, and other outdoor activities.

The parents and families in Ariel were so impressed with their kids' attitudes and what they experienced that Ron Nachman and his city encouraged Bruce and Heather Johnston to help develop the Ariel National Leadership Development Center. As we took these kids into our hearts and homes—and sent our kids to Israel through the exchange program—our investment in Israel grew more personal. Many of the families and their students developed deep friendships that have continued for years.

The program expanded to include students from Nazareth, Botrus Mansour's hometown (see more about Botrus in chapter 7). Now a unique bond has been established between Americans and Israelis, including Americans and Arab believers.

The Joshua Fund

As I mentioned earlier, Joel Rosenberg taught me the importance of recognizing the needs of both the Jewish and Arab communities of Israel. He and his wife, Lynn, oversee the Joshua Fund, which recently launched Operation Epicenter, a multiyear relief strategy to bless Israel and her neighbors in the name of Jesus. The Joshua Fund provides food, clothing, medical assistance, and other supplies to the needy as well as to victims of war. The work of the fund reaches thousands of Israelis, Palestinians, Lebanese, Iraqis, and others who suffer from violence.[2]

Nazareth Baptist School

Established in 1937 and now headed by my friend Botrus Mansour, the Nazareth Baptist School is an outstanding evangelical school in the Israeli school system. Its strong reputation for academics draws more than a thousand students from kindergarten through twelfth grade. Even though NBS offers chapel services and Bible classes, more than 20 percent of the students are Muslim; 80 percent of the students are from Christian homes. Many of the graduates go on to play key roles in the Arab and Israeli communities. The Nehemiah Project supports and prays for this remarkable school and its influence on the young people of Israel.

Hope for Ishmael

Tass Saada is the director of Hope for Ishmael. Tass is a former PLO operative but now is dedicated to peace and reconciliation between Arabs and Jews. He is convinced that the answer to the turmoil in the Middle East is not political but spiritual. He is a living testimony of the power of Jesus to change hearts and lives. The Nehemiah Project endorses and supports Hope for Ishmael, which works to build a bridge of hope and love through education, cultural understanding, and faith in Jesus.[3] (See more about Saada in chapter 7.)

Forward Blessings

Two thousand years ago the apostle Paul, a Pharisee among Pharisees before his conversion, made plain the debt that Gentile Christians owe to the Jews.

> But now I am going to Jerusalem to minister to the saints. For it pleased those from Macedonia and Achaia to make a certain contribution for the poor among the saints who are in Jerusalem. It pleased them indeed, and they are their debtors. For if the Gentiles have been partakers of their spiritual things, their duty is also to minister to them in material things. (Romans 15:25–27)

Blessing Israel, according to Paul, is part of our duty, not bound in legalism, but in love. One story that has inspired me to follow through with this sacred duty is this story of Burkina Faso.

An unlikely, small, and poor country in Africa, Burkina Faso has witnessed the miracle of God's blessing people who bless Israel. A church planter named Ram Zango believed what he read in the Bible, especially passages such as Romans 9–11.

He traveled to almost four hundred churches to share the Scriptures and to ask Christians to pray for Israel. Soon hundreds of believers in Burkina Faso were not only praying but also taking up special offerings. They even set up a House of Israel, a little mud house with an Israeli flag, where people went every day to pray for the Jewish people.

The special offerings were mailed, in faith, to the Israeli government. Eventually someone asked where these checks were coming from and began to investigate why a people who could barely feed their own families would send money to Israel. The government leaders were so touched by this support that they sent an agricultural expert to Burkina Faso to offer his expertise in growing crops and to set up programs to feed the hungry people of the tiny nation.

In October 2009 additional special aid was sent by the Israeli Ministry of Foreign Affairs and the Joint Distribution Committee to Burkina Faso. The West African country had recently suffered damaging floods. Hundreds of thousands of people had become refugees in their own country. The ministry, through MASHAV (Israel's National Agency for International Cooperation) and in cooperation with the Joint Distribution Committee, sent the country tents, blankets, medicine, and baby food. "Burkina Faso, which is a member of the UN Security Council, is one of Israel's most loyal friends in Africa," says the Israeli Ministry of Foreign Affairs.[4]

These are a people who literally believe God's promise when He said to Abraham, "I will bless those who bless you" (Genesis 12:3). These are blessed, historic, exciting times. These are the days when we see the Bible coming true before our eyes, and we are invited, indeed beckoned by God, to be part of the story.

Back to Jerusalem

The Great Commission (see Matthew 28:18–20) gives the church a defining mission. But for our generation that mission has been enlarged to include a nation that, until recently, did not even exist.

Christianity was born in Jerusalem, emerging from the Jewish faith to proclaim that the Messiah had come. Built upon a foundation of centuries of faith in the One

True God, the church sprang from its Jewish roots, became a worldwide influential force, and then too quickly forgot her heritage. Politics, power struggles, ignorance, and deception gnawed at those Jewish roots, severing the church from her foundation. Though the Jews are God's chosen people, they became the target of persecution and bigotry. Replacement theology proclaimed that the church had emerged as God's new chosen people, relegating Israel to the garbage heap of history. But in 1948, when Israel became a nation again, the church was forced to rethink centuries of ignoring or resisting its Jewish ancestry.

After Jesus's resurrection, He gave us specific instructions: "But you shall receive power when the Holy Spirit has come upon you; and you shall be witnesses to Me in Jerusalem, and in all Judea and Samaria, and to the end of the earth" (Acts 1:8). Again, it all starts in Jerusalem. Figuratively and literally. The traditional interpretation is that we are to minister first in Jerusalem, our immediate community; next, Judea, representing our larger city; then Samaria, our nation—and on to the rest of the world. I agree. The church is called to help with discipleship and church planting, providing resources and encouragement to help churches in other nations build their own communities.

I also take Jesus's words literally. We are to literally, physically, take the gospel to Jerusalem, Judea, Samaria, and the ends of the earth. Bible teacher Mark Biltz adds, "First and foremost, the commandment to start in Jerusalem still applies today even before we take the spiritual leap in correctly applying it also to our own Jerusalem. This doesn't do away with the literal command." He goes on to ask how many churches have outreaches in Israel, then adds, "Maybe it was for the best that there haven't been too many until we are ready to show mercy and grace!"[5]

The church is slowly awakening to its true heritage, to its calling to bless Israel and respond to God's invitation to help restore His people: "See, I will beckon to the Gentiles, I will lift up my banner to the peoples; they will bring your sons in their arms and carry your daughters on their shoulders" (Isaiah 49:22, NIV). This chapter in Isaiah is a beautiful expression of God comforting a desolate and frightened people, promising them restoration and blessing. Thousands of years ago He said that He would use Gentiles, like you and me, to fulfill His promises.

God is restoring Israel, and He is using His body of believers around the world. He is restoring His people—the nation He created, a people of His own—to their former glory.

We have an opportunity to replace centuries of replacement theology, persecution, neglect, and ignorance—and to do this with love and gratitude. We can help wash away the pain that has shadowed and often embittered God's chosen people. We can take to heart the words of Paul: "I am not ashamed of the gospel, because it is the power of God for the salvation of everyone who believes: first for the Jew, then for the Gentile" (Romans 1:16, NIV). We start with Jerusalem and pray that they will know their Messiah and discover the church to be a place of blessing, not an institution to fear. We honor God when we honor His people, and we are blessed when we bless them.

The gospel was born in Jerusalem. Now it is time to bring it home.

RECOMMENDED READING

Biltz, Mark. *The Feasts of the Lord* (DVD set). Bonney Lake, WA: El Shaddai Ministries, 2008.

Bullinger, E. W. *Witness of the Stars*. 1893, reprint, Grand Rapids, MI: Kregel, 1967.

Doyle, Tom. *Dreams and Visions: Is Jesus Awakening the Muslim World?* Nashville, TN: Thomas Nelson, 2012.

Finto, Don. *Your People Shall Be My People*. Ventura, CA: Regal Books, 2001.

Fruchtenbaum, Arnold. *Footsteps of the Messiah*. San Antonio, TX: Ariel Ministries, 2003.

Gilder, George. *The Israel Test*. Minneapolis, MN: Richard Vigilante Books, 2009.

Gruber, Daniel. *The Church and the Jews*. Hanover, NH: Elijah Publishing, 1997.

Gruber, Daniel. *Copernicus and the Jews*. Hanover, NH: Elijah Publishing, 2005.

Gruber, Daniel. "Elijahnet: For the Redemption of Israel," www.elijahnet.net.

Howard, Kevin, and Marvin Rosenthal. *The Feasts of the Lord*. Nashville, TN: Thomas Nelson, 1997).

Kennedy, D. James. *The Real Meaning of the Zodiac*. Fort Lauderdale, FL: Coral Ridge Ministries, 1989.

Luther, Martin. *Commentary on Romans*. Translated by J. Theodore Mueller. Grand Rapids, MI: Kregel, 1976.

Mansour, Botrus. *When Your Neighbor Is the Savior*. Pasadena, CA: Hope Publishing, 2011.

Mawire, Robert. *The Global Dilemma*. Fort Worth, TX: Robert Mawire, 2011.

Rosenberg, Joel C. *Epicenter*. Carol Stream, IL: Tyndale, 2006.

Saada, Tass. *Once an Arafat Man: The True Story of How a PLO Sniper Found a New Life*. Carol Stream, IL: Tyndale, 2008.

Wirt, Sherwood E. *Faith's Heroes*. Westchester, IL: Cornerstone Books, 1979.

Introduction: These Are the People the Prophets Saw

1. Harriet Sherwood, "Israel: Air strikes were 'against Hezbollah and not the Syrian regime,'" *The Guardian,* May 6, 2013, www.guardian.co.uk/world/2013/may/06/israel-syria-air-strikes-assad-government.

Chapter 2: Joining Today's Developments in an Ancient Story

1. Scott Harrison, "Beach Baptism," *Los Angeles Times,* May 6, 1973, http://framework.latimes.com/2011/02/15/beach-baptism.
2. Sherwood Eliot Wirt, *For the Love of Mike* (Nashville, TN: Thomas Nelson, 1984), 93.
3. John Wesley and Charles Wesley, *John and Charles Wesley: Selected Prayers, Hymns, Journal Notes, Sermons, Letters and Treatises,* edited by Emilie Griffin (New York: Paulist Press, 1981), 107.
4. "The Future of the Global Muslim Population," Pew Research Religion & Public Life Project, January 27, 2011, www.pewforum.org/2011/01/27/the-future-of-the-global-muslim-population.
5. See "Ancient Jewish History: The Two Kingdoms," Jewish Virtual Library, www.jewishvirtuallibrary.org/jsource/History/Kingdoms1.html.

Chapter 3: God's Covenant with Abraham Remains Fully in Force

1. Robert Mawire, *The Global Dilemma* (Fort Worth, TX: Robert Mawire, 2011), 1.
2. "Shechem," Jewish Virtual Library, www.jewishvirtuallibrary.org/jsource/Society_&_Culture/geo/Shechem.html.

Chapter 4: Restoring the Glory of the Holy Land

1. Blue Letter Bible, "Dictionary and Word Search for mazzarah (Strong's 4216)," Blue Letter Bible, 1996–2013, www.blueletterbible.org/lang/lexicon/lexicon.cfm?Strongs=H4216&t=KJV.

2. Daniel Gruber, *The Separation of Church and Faith,* vol. 1: *Copernicus and the Jews* (Hanover, NH: Elijah Publishing, 2005), 123.

Chapter 5: A Personal Introduction to an Unlikely Prophet
1. Leah Abramowitz, "The Jerusalem Syndrome," Jewish Virtual Library, www .jewishvirtuallibrary.org/jsource/History/jersynd.html.
2. This is how the agreement was characterized by Cable News Network (CNN), "Struggle for Peace: A Chronology of Recent Events in the Middle East," www .cnn.com/world/struggle_for_peace/background.

Chapter 6: An Ancient Gentile Points the Way
1. Maurice Samuel, *You Gentiles* (New York: Harcourt, Brace & Co., 1924), 9.
2. See L. Grant Hutton, *In His Own Words: Messianic Insights into the Hebrew Alphabet* (Hartville, OH: Beth Tikkun, 1999). Mark Biltz recommended I read this book on the Hebrew alphabet.
3. Jewish tradition says Samuel wrote the book of Judges, but we don't know for sure.
4. See "An Introduction to Judaism, Jewish Conversion, and Converting to Judaism," Conversion to Judaism, www.convertingtojudaism.com.

Chapter 7: Learning from the Descendants of Ishmael
1. Moshe Dayan, quoted in Avi Shlaim, *The Iron Wall: Israel and the Arab World* (New York: Norton, 2001), 101.
2. Botrus Mansour, *When Your Neighbor Is the Savior* (Pasadena, CA: Hope Publishing House, 2011), 94.
3. Tass Saada, *Once an Arafat Man* (Wheaton, IL: Tyndale House, 2008), 27.
4. Joel Rosenberg on Madeline Albright, citing Michael Dobbs, "Albright's Family Tragedy Comes to Light," *Washington Post,* February 4, 1997, www .washingtonpost.com/wp-srv/politics/govt/admin/stories/albright020497.htm.

Chapter 8: History's Most Persecuted People
1. For more on this, see Daniel Gruber, *The Church and the Jews* (Hanover, NH: Elijah Publishing, 1997), 19.
2. Gruber, *Church and the Jews,* 19.

3. Justin Martyr, *Dialogue with Trypho,* translated by A. Lukyn Williams (London: SPCK, 1930), 33–34, sec. 16.4, quoted in Gruber, *The Church and the Jews,* 28.

4. Justin Martyr, *Dialogue with Trypho,* 169, sec. 80.1–5, quoted in Gruber, *The Church and the Jews,* 29.

5. Gruber, *Church and the Jews,* 17.

6. For more, see Eusebius of Caesarea, *Ecclesiastical History,* translated by Christian Frederick Cruse (Grand Rapids, MI: Baker Book, 1989), e.g. *Book of Martyrs,* chap. 11, 369.

7. Jean Juster, *Les Juifs dan l'empire romain: leur condition juridique, économique et sociale* I (*The Jews in the Roman Empire*) (Paris: Geuthner, 1914), 308ff, quoted in C. W. Dugmore, "A Note on the Quartodecimans," *Studia Patristica* 4 (1961): 410–21, quoted in Gruber, *The Church and the Jews,* 31.

8. Eusebius, *Ecclesiastical History,* 51–54.

9. Isaac Boyle, "A Historical View of the Council of Nicea" [1850], in Eusebius, *Ecclesiastical History,* 27, quoted in Gruber, *The Church and the Jews,* 37.

10. Sherwood Eliot Wirt, *Faith's Heroes: A Fresh Look at Ten Great Christians* (Westchester, IL: Cornerstone, 1979), 51.

11. For more, see "Martin Luther (1483–1546): Theologian of the Holocaust," *Jerusalem Post,* July 22, 2011, blogs.jpost.com/content/martin-luther-1483 -1546-theologian-holocaust, as well as numerous other sources.

12. Martin Luther, *Commentary on Romans,* translated by J. Theodore Mueller (1954, reprint, Grand Rapids: MI: Kregel, 1976), 156.

13. Martin Luther, *The Jews and Their Lies* (1543, reprint, York, SC: Liberty Bell Publisher, 2004), 16.

14. Luther, *Commentary on Romans,* 162.

15. Luther, *Jews and Their Lies,* 37–43.

16. For more, see William Nicholls, *Christian Antisemitism: A History of Hate* (Lanham, MD: Rowman & Littlefield, 1993), 270–71.

17. Adolf Hitler, *Mein Kampf* ("My Struggle"), translated by Ralph Manheim (1943, reprint, New York: Mariner Books, 1999), 65.

Chapter 9: Tracing Israel's Destiny Through the Ninth Day of Av

1. See Andrea Stone, "Gaza settlers leave home behind," August 14, 2005, http:// usatoday30.usatoday.com/news/world/2005-08-14-gaza-cover_x.htm.

2. Sara Yoheved Rigler, "Tisha B'Av: Waking Up to a World without God's Presence," aish.com, July 7, 2005, www.aish.com/h/9av/ju/48936167.html.
3. Shraga Simmons, "Tisha B'Av—The Ninth of Av," aish.com, June 19, 2002, www.aish.com/h/9av/oal/48944076.html.
4. See Simmons, "Tisha B'Av—The Ninth of Av," www.aish.com/h/9av/oal/48944076.html.

Chapter 10: Meeting the Israelis from Ezekiel's Prophecy

1. "Intifada Toll 2000–2005," BBC News, February 8, 2005, http://news.bbc.co.uk/2/hi/middle_east/3694350.stm. See also Ziv Hellman, "The Second Intifada Begins," My Jewish Learning, www.myjewishlearning.com/israel/Contemporary_Life/Israeli-Palestinian_Relations/Second_Intifada.shtml.
2. See "Occasions: The 29th of November," www.knesset.gov.il/holidays/eng/29nov_e.htm.
3. The word *Zionism* was coined in 1890 to describe the "national movement for the return of the Jewish people to their homeland and the resumption of Jewish sovereignty in the land of Israel"; see "Zionism: A Definition of Zionism," www.jewishvirtuallibrary.org/jsource/Zionism/zionism.html.

Chapter 11: Israel's Once and Future Leader

1. Audio recording of Benjamin Netanyahu's address delivered April 16, 2001, in Fort Lauderdale, Florida, available at http://media.calvaryftl.org/archive/index.cfm?sortby=date&sortorder=desc&showycarsfilter=1&showbiblebooksfilter=1&showspeakersfilter=1&showministriesfilter=1&showcampusesfilter=1&showtopicsfilter=0&showseriesfilter=1&per_page=20&speaker=Benjamin+Netanyahu&book=&yr=.

Chapter 12: Patterns and Predictions in Prophecy

1. J. Vernon McGee, *Thru the Bible with J. Vernon McGee,* 6 vols. (Nashville, TN: Thomas Nelson, 1981–98), 3:332.
2. See Chuck Missler, "Midrash Hermeneutics," Koinonia House, May 2001, http://www.khouse.org/articles/2001/341.
3. James Strong, *Abingdon's Strong's Exhaustive Concordance of the Bible* (1894, reprint, Nashville, TN: Abingdon, 1986), 434; entry to *A Concise Dictionary of the Words in the Greek/New Testament,* G5179, 98.

4. Robert Mawire, *The Global Dilemma* (Fort Worth, TX: Robert Mawire, 2011), 21.
5. Joel C. Rosenberg, "Israeli Newspaper Reports 15,000 Jewish Believers in Jesus in Israel: 350,000 in the U.S.," *Joel C. Rosenberg's Blog* (blog), August 20, 2010, http://flashtrafficblog.wordpress.com/2010/08/20/israeli-newspaper-says-15000 -jewish-belivers-in-jesus-in-israel-350000-in-the-u-s.
6. "Address by PM Netanyahu at Auschwitz concentration camp," Israel Ministry of Foreign Affairs, January 27, 2010, www.mfa.gov.il/MFA/Government /Speeches+by+Israeli+leaders/2010/Address_PM_Netanyahu_at_Auschwitz _27-Jan-2010.htm. The prime minister was paraphrasing Ezekiel 37:4–11.
7. Ron Nachman, quoted in Tovah Lazaroff, "Ariel Founder Ron Nachman to be buried," *Jerusalem Post,* January 20, 2013, www.jpost.com/National-News /Ariel-founder-Ron-Nachman-to-be-buried.

Chapter 13: What God's Signs in the Heavens Tell Us

1. Blue Letter Bible, "Dictionary and Word Search for mazzarah (Strong's 4216)," Blue Letter Bible, 1996–2013, www.blueletterbible.org/lang/lexicon/lexicon .cfm? Strongs=H4216&t=KJV.
2. James Strong, *Abingdon's Strong's Exhaustive Concordance of the Bible* (1894, reprint, Nashville, TN: Abingdon, 1986), 11, Hebrew dictionary section, ref. 226.
3. See D. James Kennedy, *The Real Meaning of the Zodiac,* compiled and edited by Nancy Britt (Fort Lauderdale, FL: Coral Ridge Ministries, 1989), 8.
4. See E. W. Bullinger, *The Witness of the Stars* (1893, reprint, Grand Rapids, MI: Kregel, 1967), 10.
5. Flavius Josephus, *The Life and Works of Flavius Josephus,* translated by William Whiston (London: Bowyer, 1737), 1.2.36.
6. For more on this, see E. A. Wallis Budge, *Babylonian Life and History* (1886, reprint, New York: Barnes & Noble, 2005).
7. See Aratus, *Phaenomena,* Cambridge Classic Texts and Commentaries, no. 34 (Cambridge: Cambridge University Press, 2004).
8. See Kennedy, *Real Meaning of the Zodiac,* 12.
9. See also Strong, *Abingdon's Strong's Exhaustive Concordance,* ref. 5476, page 108, *Hebrew and Chaldee Dictionary.*
10. "Ancient Jewish History: The Twelve Tribes of Israel," Jewish Virtual Library, www.jewishvirtuallibrary.org/jsource/Judaism/tribes.html.

Chapter 14: The Riddle of the Sphinx

1. Flavius Josephus, *The Life and Works of Flavius Josephus,* translated by William Whiston (London: Bowyer, 1737), 1.9.74.
2. See D. James Kennedy, *The Real Meaning of the Zodiac,* compiled and edited by Nancy Britt (Fort Lauderdale, FL: Coral Ridge Ministries, 1989), 19.
3. See E. W. Bullinger, *The Witness of the Stars* (1893, reprint, Grand Rapids, MI: Kregel, 1967), 18. There are several interpretations regarding which tribes of Israel are associated with which signs of the zodiac. Bullinger's interpretation makes the most sense and is the most biblically grounded.
4. See Isaiah 11:1 (Vulgate), cited in Bullinger, *Witness of the Stars,* 30.
5. Bullinger, *Witness of the Stars,* 54.
6. Bullinger, *Witness of the Stars,* 63.

Chapter 15: The Zodiac and Christ's Second Coming

1. Just because followers of the occult twisted early astronomy into astrology does not diminish the fact that the images found in the familiar constellations represent biblical themes and help broadcast the truth of God and His Son.
2. See David Guzik, "Study Guide for Revelation 5," *Enduring Word, Blue Letter Bible,* July 7, 2006; www.blueletterbible.org/commentaries/comm_view.cfm?AuthorID=2&contentID=8107&commInfo=31&topic=Revelation.

Chapter 16: How Seasons and Feasts Reveal Christ's Second Coming

1. James Strong, *Abingdon's Strong's Exhaustive Concordance of the Bible* (1894, reprint, Nashville, TN: Abingdon, 1986), 83, ref. 4150, *Hebrew and Chaldee Dictionary.*
2. Strong, *Strong's Exhaustive Concordance,* 94, refs. 4744, 7121, *Hebrew and Chaldee Dictionary.*
3. Marvin Rosenthal and Kevin Howard, *The Feasts of the Lord* (Nashville, TN: Thomas Nelson, 1997), 13.
4. See Rosenthal and Howard, *The Feasts of the Lord,* 13.

Chapter 17: Prophetic Truth Found in the Fall Feasts of the Jewish Calendar

1. Zola Levitt, *The Seven Feasts of Israel* (Dallas, TX: Zola Levitt Ministries, 1979, 2012), 12.
2. See Marvin Rosenthal and Kevin Howard, *The Feasts of the Lord* (Nashville, TN: Thomas Nelson, 1997), 105.
3. James Strong, *Abingdon's Strong's Exhaustive Concordance of the Bible* (1894, reprint, Nashville, TN: Abingdon, 1986), 54, ref. 2646, from 2645, *Hebrew and Chaldee Dictionary.* The prophet Joel referred to a private room, which is the Hebrew word *chuppah,* or canopy.
4. See Edward Chumney, *The Seven Festivals of the Messiah* (Shippensburg, PA: Treasure House, 1994), 138–39.
5. See Alfred Edersheim, *The Temple: Its Ministry and Services as They Were at the Time of Jesus Christ* (1874, reprint, Grand Rapids, MI: Kregel, 1997).
6. See Rosenthal and Howard, *Feasts of the Lord,* 127.
7. See Rosenthal and Howard, *Feasts of the Lord,* 135.

Chapter 18: The Feasts Still Open Our Eyes to God

1. Nicholas Boyle, *2014: How to Survive the Next World Crisis* (London and New York: Continuum, 2010), quoted in "Cambridge Professor: 2014 Pivotal for Disaster," Dark Government, www.darkgovernment.com/news/cambridge -professor-2014-pivotal-for-disaster.
2. Boyle, *2014,* 5.
3. "Basel Program," Jewish Encyclopedia, www.jewishencyclopedia.com/articles /2612-basel-program.
4. "Theodor (Binyamin Ze'ev) Herzl," Jewish Virtual Library, www.jewishvirtual library.org/jsource/biography/Herzl.html.
5. Arnold G. Fruchtenbaum, *Footsteps of the Messiah: A Study of the Sequence of Prophetic Events,* rev. ed. (Tusin, CA: Ariel Ministries, 2003), 437.
6. See Marvin Rosenthal and Kevin Howard, *The Feasts of the Lord* (Nashville, TN: Thomas Nelson, 1997), 159–60.
7. "The Welsh Revival: Effects of 1904 Revival," www.welshrevival.com.
8. Philip Jenkins, *The Next Christendom: The Coming of Global Christianity,* 3rd ed. (New York: Oxford University Press, 2011), 2–3.

9. See Joel C. Rosenberg, *Inside the Revolution* (Carol Stream, IL: Tyndale, 2009), 433.

Chapter 19: Daniel's Seventy Weeks

1. See Chuck Smith, *Word for Today Bible,* Commentary, Daniel (Nashville, TN: Thomas Nelson, 2005), 1123.
2. See Chuck Missler, "The Precision of Prophecy: Daniel's 70 Weeks," Koinonia House, www.khouse.org/articles/2004/552.
3. Larry Norman, "I Wish We'd All Been Ready," Lyrics EMI Music Publishing, 1969.
4. J. Vernon McGee, *Thru the Bible with J. Vernon McGee,* 6 vols. (Nashville, TN: Thomas Nelson, 1981–98), 3:332.
5. See Cecil Maranville, "The Kingdom of God: The Heart of Christ's Message," *The Good News,* www.ucg.org/doctrinal-beliefs/kingdom-god-heart-christs -message.
6. There are numerous Internet sources for this story, and apparently it has become part of the lectures given by tour guides in Rome. See Sarina Roffé, "A Historical Background of Italian Jewry: Jews Built Roman Coliseum After Destruction of Second Temple," www.jewishgen.org/sephardic/coliseum.htm.

Chapter 20: How NASA Research Clarifies Biblical Prophecy

1. For more on blood moons and tetrads, see NASA Eclipse Web Site, National Aeronautics and Space Administration, http://eclipse.gsfc.nasa.gov/eclipse.html.
2. Talmud, Mas. Sukkah 29a, http://halakhah.com/pdf/moed/Sukkah.pdf.
3. See Rabbi Ken Spiro, "History Crash Course #48: The Inquisition," Aish.com, www.aish.com/jl/h/48951681.html.
4. Henry Ford, *The International Jew: The World's Foremost Problem* (1920, reprint; Whitefish, MT: Kessinger Publishing, 2003), 33. See also Henry Ford, *The International Jew: The World's Foremost Problem,* Internet Archive: Digital Library of Free Books, Movies, Music & Wayback Machine, http://archive.org /details/TheInternationalJewTheWorldsForemostProblemhenryFord1920s.
5. See "Christopher Columbus (1451–1506)," Jewish-American Hall of Fame, www.amuseum.org/jahf/virtour/index.html#columbus.

6. See "Modern Jewish History: The Spanish Expulsion (1492)," www.jewish virtuallibrary.org/jsource/Judaism/expulsion.html.

7. See Eliezer Segal, "Columbus's Medinah?" From the Sources, Jewish Free Press, October 14, 1991, http://people.ucalgary.ca/~elsegal/Shokel/911014_Columbus .html.

8. Christopher Columbus, ed., *The Book of Prophecies,* vol. 3, *Repertorium Colum-bianum,* ed. Roberto Rusconi, trans. Blair Sullivan (Eugene, OR: Wipf & Stock, 2004), 18–19.

9. See Chuck Missler, "Mysteries Behind Our History: Was Columbus Jewish?" (1996), Koinonia House, www.khouse.org/articles/1996/109.

10. Columbus, *Book of Prophecies,* 3:20.

11. Columbus, *Book of Prophecies,* 3:229.

12. Columbus, *Book of Prophecies,* 3:24.

13. Columbus, *Book of Prophecies,* Introduction, 33.

14. Augustine of Hippo, quoted in Columbus, *Book of Prophecies,* 3:163.

Chapter 21: God Is Bringing His People Home

1. "Declaration of the Establishment of the State of Israel, May 14, 1948," Israel Ministry of Foreign Affairs, www.mfa.gov.il/mfa/foreignpolicy/peace/guide /pages/declaration%20of%20establishment%20of%20state%20of%20israel .aspx.

2. "Aliyah, October 29, 2002," Israel Ministry of Foreign Affairs, http://mfa.gov.il /MFA/MFA-Archive/2002/Pages/Aliyah.aspx.

3. George Gilder, *The Israel Test* (Minneapolis, MN: Richard Vigilante Books, 2009), 30.

4. See Stephen M. Wylen, *The Seventy Faces of Torah: The Jewish Way of Reading the Sacred Scriptures* (New York: Paulist Press, 2005). See also John J. Parsons, "Seventy Faces of Torah: Brief Overview of Jewish Exegesis," *Hebrew for Chris-tians,* www.hebrew4christians.com/Articles/Seventy_Faces/seventy_faces.html.

Chapter 22: Rebuilding the Heart of the Holy Land

1. See Maranatha Chapel, www.maranathachapel.org/ministries/nehemiah -project/new-page/american-friends-of-ariel.

2. For more about the Joshua Fund, see www.joshuafund.net.

3. For more about Hope for Ishmael, see http://nowsprouting.com/hope forishmael.

4. "Israel Sends Aid to Flood-Stricken Burkina Faso," October 13, 2009, Israel Ministry of Foreign Affairs, www.mfa.gov.il/mfa/pressroom/2009/pages /israeli_aid_to_burkina_faso_13_oct_2009.aspx.

5. These quotes are from a personal conversation with Mark Biltz, Ray Bentley, and Genevieve Gillespie.